Deleuze's Philosophy of Law

Plateaus – New Directions in Deleuze Studies

'It's not a matter of bringing all sorts of things together under a single concept but rather of relating each concept to variables that explain its mutations.'
Gilles Deleuze, *Negotiations*

Series Editors
Ian Buchanan, University of Wollongong
Claire Colebrook, Penn State University

Editorial Advisory Board
Keith Ansell Pearson, Ronald Bogue, Constantin V. Boundas, Rosi Braidotti, Eugene Holland, Gregg Lambert, Dorothea Olkowski, Paul Patton, Daniel Smith, James Williams

Titles available in the series
Christian Kerslake, *Immanence and the Vertigo of Philosophy: From Kant to Deleuze*
Jean-Clet Martin, *Variations: The Philosophy of Gilles Deleuze*, translated by Constantin V. Boundas and Susan Dyrkton
Simone Bignall, *Postcolonial Agency: Critique and Constructivism*
Miguel de Beistegui, *Immanence – Deleuze and Philosophy*
Jean-Jacques Lecercle, *Badiou and Deleuze Read Literature*
Ronald Bogue, *Deleuzian Fabulation and the Scars of History*
Sean Bowden, *The Priority of Events: Deleuze's Logic of Sense*
Craig Lundy, *History and Becoming: Deleuze's Philosophy of Creativity*
Aidan Tynan, *Deleuze's Literary Clinic: Criticism and the Politics of Symptoms*
Thomas Nail, *Returning to Revolution: Deleuze, Guattari and Zapatismo*
François Zourabichvili, *Deleuze: A Philosophy of the Event* with *The Vocabulary of Deleuze* edited by Gregg Lambert and Daniel W. Smith, translated by Kieran Aarons
Frida Beckman, *Between Desire and Pleasure: A Deleuzian Theory of Sexuality*
Nadine Boljkovac, *Untimely Affects: Gilles Deleuze and an Ethics of Cinema*
Daniela Voss, *Conditions of Thought: Deleuze and Transcendental Ideas*
Daniel Barber, *Deleuze and the Naming of God: Post-Secularism and the Future of Immanence*
F. LeRon Shults, *Iconoclastic Theology: Gilles Deleuze and the Secretion of Atheism*
Janae Sholtz, *The Invention of a People: Heidegger and Deleuze on Art and the Political*
Marco Altamirano, *Time, Technology and Environment: An Essay on the Philosophy of Nature*
Sean McQueen, *Deleuze and Baudrillard: From Cyberpunk to Biopunk*
Ridvan Askin, *Narrative and Becoming*
Marc Rölli, *Gilles Deleuze's Transcendental Empiricism: From Tradition to Difference*, translated by Peter Hertz-Ohmes
Guillaume Collett, *The Psychoanalysis of Sense: Deleuze and the Lacanian School*
Ryan J. Johnson, *The Deleuze-Lucretius Encounter*
Allan James Thomas, *Deleuze, Cinema and the Thought of the World*
Cheri Lynne Carr, *Deleuze's Kantian Ethos: Critique as a Way of Life*
Alex Tissandier, *Affirming Divergence: Deleuze's Reading of Leibniz*
Barbara Glowczewski, *Indigenising Anthropology with Guattari and Deleuze*
Koichiro Kokubun, *The Principles of Deleuzian Philosophy*, translated by Wren Nishina
Felice Cimatti, *Unbecoming Human: Philosophy of Animality After Deleuze*, translated by Fabio Gironi
Ryan J. Johnson, *Deleuze, A Stoic*
Jane Newland, *Deleuze in Children's Literature*
D. J. S. Cross, *Deleuze and the Problem of Affect*
Laurent de Sutter, *Deleuze's Philosophy of Law*, translated by Nils F. Schott

Forthcoming volumes
Justin Litaker, *Deleuze and Guattari's Political Economy*
Nir Kedem, *A Deleuzian Critique of Queer Thought: Overcoming Sexuality*
Sean Bowden, *Expression, Action and Agency in Deleuze: Willing Events*
Andrew Jampol-Petzinger, *Deleuze, Kierkegaard and the Ethics of Selfhood*

Visit the Plateaus website at edinburghuniversitypress.com/series/plat

DELEUZE'S PHILOSOPHY OF LAW

Laurent de Sutter

Translated by Nils F. Schott

EDINBURGH
University Press

Edinburgh University Press is one of the leading university presses in the UK. We publish academic books and journals in our selected subject areas across the humanities and social sciences, combining cutting-edge scholarship with high editorial and production values to produce academic works of lasting importance. For more information visit our website: edinburghuniversitypress.com

Originally published in France under the title *Deleuze. La Pratique du droit*
Copyright © Laurent de Sutter, Michalon Éditeur, 2009
www.michalon.fr

English translation © Nils F. Schott, 2022, 2023

Edinburgh University Press Ltd
The Tun – Holyrood Road, 12(2f) Jackson's Entry, Edinburgh EH8 8PJ

First published in hardback by Edinburgh University Press 2022

Typeset in 11/13 Sabon LT Std by
Cheshire Typesetting Ltd, Cuddington, Cheshire, and
printed and bound by CPI Group (UK) Ltd,
Croydon, CR0 4YY

A CIP record for this book is available from the British Library

ISBN 978 1 4744 0832 5 (hardback)
ISBN 978 1 3995 2240 3 (paperback)
ISBN 978 1 4744 0833 2 (webready PDF)
ISBN 978 1 4744 0834 9 (epub)

Contents

Note

This book contains a complete exposition of Gilles Deleuze's philosophy of law. Since, as will become apparent, this philosophy is characterised by its great autonomy from the axioms of Deleuze's system in general, the present volume does not offer an introduction to Deleuze's system. For interested readers, the bibliography lists works that offer such an introduction.

Preface to the English Edition

1 Reconstruction This book lays out a reconstruction of the kind police detectives and archaeologists perform, whose task is to reconstruct, on the basis of a few dispersed clues, the totality of a sequence of facts – or the totality of an object, a place, or a civilisation now vanished. The reconstitution at issue in this book concerns such an object, which also belongs to a past that, for all its proximity, is no less difficult to decipher: Gilles Deleuze's philosophy of law. As is the case in archaeology, its material is an enigmatic set of traces scattered amidst other, heterogeneous material. And its goal, as in the case of police investigations, is to attribute the facts that constitute a crime to an individual who has done everything to conceal its traces. What you will find in this book is thus none other than a puzzle: the result of gathering (almost) all the instances in Deleuze's texts where he makes reference to law as well as a risky attempt at organising them, a puzzle whose only advantage is that it at least includes the totality of these occurrences, (almost) without exception. Nonetheless, and despite its risky nature, such a reconstruction is authorised by declarations by Deleuze himself, with implications even for his personal biography, as you will see in the introduction. However exclusive his passion for philosophy may have been, it left space for a regret, or a fantasy: what would have happened, Deleuze wondered, had I not gone into philosophy but into law? The answer, such as it emerges in these pages, is simple and crystal clear: he would no doubt still have done philosophy.

2 *Use*   Since this book was first published in October 2009, a number of works in various languages have been devoted to the traces I try to put together and articulate here. Whatever their quality (I discuss some of them in Appendix 2), it is a fact that to this day, none has tried to replicate the exercise I propose in these pages. The reason might be that the increasing interest in Deleuze's philosophy of law is coming from jurists and not from philosophers – an interest guided by the wish to invent, thanks to Deleuze, new ways of thinking and practising the law. As Deleuze himself suggested, such work, rather than lose precious time on exegeses and commentaries, claims to make *use* of his thinking in this or that area of the law, as if his philosophy were a toolbox. While this claim is perfectly legitimate, the *power* of uses nonetheless depends on the power of the tools they create – and thus on the materials they make use of in such a creation. Whether it belongs to the world of theory or to the world of practice (in law, that amounts to the same), inventing a use of Deleuze's philosophy likely to open up new juridical becomings requires, first of all, *fabricating* a useful Deleuze. The intention of this book, like the ambition to be exhaustive that animates it, is thus to fabricate the most powerful Deleuze possible such that the invention of new juridical uses on the basis of his thinking becomes so much easier. The *petitio principii* of this book is that Deleuze's philosophy of law comes to bear more through its system than through its theses – that is to say, it applies more through the *connection* of the theses taken together than through the *conjugation* of each of them taken separately.

3 *System*   This *petitio principii* rests on the equally biased assumption that Deleuze's thinking has *two major characteristics*: (a) its *systematicity* and (b) its *traditionalism*. This twofold characterisation has been advocated by Alain Badiou in his *Deleuze: The Clamor of Being*, a book that prompted a lot of criticism, most of it unjustified.[1] Indeed, (a) by qualifying Deleuze's thinking as *systematic*, Badiou simply put

his finger on the fact that its development took place in a continuous rather than a discontinuous manner. In Deleuze, each thesis, established first for its own sake (in the format of a paragraph), is then established in its relationship with the theses surrounding it (in the format of a chapter, then of a book). But above all, each thesis is the subject of a reprise from book to book, or from article to article: Deleuze is systematic because his thinking *persists*, albeit through the many transformations he subjects it to. What matters to him above all is *displacing* and *reinscribing* the theses close to his heart in new milieux where they can pursue their existence. Deleuze is not a systematic philosopher in the sense that his thinking would proceed from a beginning towards an end; he is a systematic philosopher to the extent that his thinking is not monographic. While it is indeed the objects that command the invention of concepts, such invention in the end always gives rise to a universe of thought adequate to the universe of the objects themselves: an absolute totality – what Badiou, employing an expression of Deleuze's, calls a 'One-All'.[2] This systematic dimension of Deleuze's oeuvre is one of the presuppositions on which my reconstruction of his philosophy of law rests (or one of the intuitions I have followed).

4 Tradition Yet Deleuze's thinking is not only systematic: it is, moreover, (b) *traditional* or 'classic' in the sense that, as Badiou also explains, it consciously inscribes itself in a certain philosophical tradition.[3] This philosophical tradition is that of French metaphysics, whose history, inaugurated by Descartes, has found some of its greatest masters among those whose lessons Deleuze followed.[4] In fact, Deleuze does not claim to be doing anything other than metaphysics – nothing else, that is, than philosophy in the purest sense of the term, even if compromises must be made as to its method or its objects. The *problems* that interest Deleuze – be they those of the relations between time and space, of sensation, or of memory – all belong to the classic corpus of problems in philosophy, including philosophy in the most scholastic sense. This is not to say, of course, that Deleuze's work could be reduced to that of a simple heir. It is, rather, to point out how much this work, when taken seriously, must be considered the work of someone for whom philosophy trumps all other considerations. Thus Deleuze's philosophy of law, if it exists, must be understood as a moment, or a variation, in a larger enterprise to which the law (like any other thing) is, ultimately, a matter of indifference. When Deleuze is writing, he is writing for philosophers, his peers – it matters little to him what those think whose practices he happens to evoke, as the famous example of the surfers shows, which still makes him smile in the *Abécédaire*, a series of interviews with Claire Parnet (*A*, C). This means that legal scholars who read Deleuze and find traces of a thinking that touches on their subject must, in constructing the use they hope to make of him, *wrest* it from him based on a problem that will forever remain foreign to him, as this little book seeks to demonstrate.

5 Coherence It is thus no surprise that the book you're about to read is academic in tone and not overly concerned with implementing the theses it expounds and articulates: that is not its goal. Its only concern is with bringing to light a stratum of thinking that very much belongs to Deleuze's oeuvre, and bringing it to light in the most rigorous, complete, and coherent manner possible. As the quote that already served as the epigraph for the first edition of this book intimates, exegetes or commentators can lay claim to no other honour than to *doing justice* to the works they treat of, supposing these works stand in need of such attention. In Deleuze's case, since he never claimed to have spoken on, about, or starting from the law as such, this need existed – which explains why the work that led to this book seemed necessary. If – in keeping with the twofold *petitio principii* (systematicity and traditionalism) mentioned earlier as well as the two rules of method you'll discover in the introduction (literalness and betrayal) – I have succeeded in fabricating something like a *powerful* Deleuze, then the work will not have been entirely in vain. For all that, attentive readers will undoubtedly find in the pages that follow a certain number of new clues that do not all belong to Deleuze's oeuvre itself and point to this or that possible use in the domain of law. Among these, there is one easily wrested from his philosophy of law: that of the necessity to be done, in law, with the idea of the Law – whether understood as legislation, as rule, or as simple norm. Law is not a matter of normativity: it is a fact without force or obligation and thus also without authority – there is no use in trying to critique or to ground this fact. It can only be described and then extended or made to bifurcate.

6 Language   To understand this point, it is necessary to employ to a distinction made in most Indo-European languages, with the notable exception of English: the one that exists between *droit* and *loi*, *ius* and *lex*, *diritto* and *legge*, *derecho* and *ley*, *recht* and *wet*, *Recht* and *Gesetz*. There is, stratified in the very history of language, a difference between a normative authority and the practice that unfolds under the constraints of this authority.[5] The critique of the Law (*loi* – Part I) in which Deleuze engages can open onto a clinic of law (*droit* – Part II) precisely because it is possible to disconnect one from the other – because the Law and law, *loi* and *droit* are not one and the same thing.[6] The consequences of this distinction are considerable, not only when it comes to philosophy (and thus to the only thing Deleuze is concerned with) but also when it comes to law in all its forms. Among the consequences worth elaborating undoubtedly figures the future course of what is called Critical Legal Studies – that is, in the most general terms, the rejection of the contemporary obscenity in legal matters. Unlike what is too often supposed, going from the critical to the clinical does not mean subscribing to the way the world goes: it implies *operating within* the way the world goes – a slow and patient labour with an eye to what in China is called 'silent transformation', as François

Jullien reminds us.[7] Rather than outlining a general agenda for reforming the law, the use this little book is hoping for is that jurists develop an understanding of consequences that requires each of them to cultivate a weasel's agility. Getting rid of the idea of the Law would thus represent the first moment of a generalised *lubrication* of law that would make controlling it impossible and oblige those who practise it finally to accept submitting to the principal demand of this practice: the demand to invent.

Notes

The epigraph is taken from *D*, 119; the translation has been modified.

1. See Badiou, *Deleuze*, 17. For an elegant and balanced critique of Badiou's book, see Bergen, 'A propos de la formule de Badiou'.
2. See Badiou, *Deleuze*, 10–11.
3. Badiou, *Deleuze*, 54–5.
4. On Deleuze's intellectual genealogy, see Bianco, 'Introduzione'.
5. See Benveniste, '*Ius* and the Oath in Rome'. See also Schiavone, *The Invention of Law in the West*.
6. Translator's Note: To convey the difference, in Deleuze, between *le droit*, *la loi*, and *la Loi*, this translation follows earlier translators in using *law*, *the Law*, and THE LAW, respectively. It also follows the not always fortunate but well-established practice of rendering substantivised adjectives as such: on the model of *the political* for *le politique*, it translates *le comique* as *the comic*, *le possible* as *the possible*, and so on. Finally, to avoid the distractions that would come with alternate terms, it renders *critique* as *critique* (rather than *criticism*, for example) and *clinique* as *clinic* (rather than *critical practice* or some such).
7. See Jullien, *The Silent Transformations*.

Acknowledgements

This short work comes out of research I conducted as a member of the Law, Science, Technology and Society Research Group in the Faculty of Law at the Vrije Universiteit Brussel under the direction of Serge Gutwirth. It owes a great deal to the latter's generosity and intelligence as well as to my exchanges over the years with Isabelle Stengers and Bruno Latour: I thank all three of them. I equally thank my colleagues Nathalie Trussart and Daniel de Beer for the intellectual help they have kept on giving during the numerous *contracts* we have already spent working together. I also thank Véronique Bergen and Jérôme Game for bibliographical advice and for the theoretical suggestions they graciously made when I presented part of this book. I thank Lissa Lincoln, David Rabouin, François Cusset, and Charles Talcott for giving the first impulse to this work when they invited me to give a talk, in June 2007, at the seminar 'Local, Vital, Legal' organised by the École Normale Supérieure, The American University of Paris, and Columbia University Reid Hall. I thank François Ost for accepting to publish the results of further work in the Summer 2008 issue of the *Revue interdisciplinaire d'études juridiques*, and Peter Fitzpatrick for his translation into English for *Law, Science & Humanities*. And finally I thank, for their opinions, readings, questions, criticisms, support, etc., Thomas Berns, Pascal Chabot, Gilles Collard, David Di Nota, Elie During, Benoît Frydman, Claude Jaeglé, Laurent Jeanpierre, Claudia Landolfi, Christophe Mincke, Frédéric Neyrat, Frank Pierobon, Rémy Russotto, David Saunders, et Vincent Van Troyen. As for Marguerite Ferry, I give her my love, because it's the best I can do.

The English version would not have seen light of day without Kyle McGee's insistence, Ian Buchanan's welcoming reception and Carol Macdonald's kindness: thanks to all three for helping to bring it into being. Thanks also to Nils F. Schott for his impeccable translation work and to Erika Weitzman who translated the original version of the chapter on the young girls that appeared in the *New York Law School Law Review* in the proceedings of the 'Visualizing Law in the Digital Age' conference organised by Richard Sherwin. In the time between its publication in French and its translation into English, this little book has also been published in Italian by Ombre Corte: for that I would like to thank Sandro Chignola, Lorenzo Rustighi and Gianfranco Morosato. Giso Amendola wrote a remarkable review of the volume for *Il Manifesto*, for which I am grateful, as I am for our subsequent exchanges via email or on social networks. Peter Goodrich honoured me with an invitation to present the book's theses at Yeshiva University's Benjamin N. Cardozo School of Law in New York in October 2011. I would like to thank him for it, as I would like to thank the participants of a roundtable on my work, in particular Nathan Moore, Jeanne Schroeder and Michel Rosenfeld. For their comments, criticism and encouragements, I would like to thank, finally, Constantin Boundas, Alexandre Lefebvre, Paul Patton and Clément Rosset. The remark – half in earnest, half in jest – in a letter from Rosset that 'if ever Deleuze had got it into his head to write about law, he would no doubt have written a book like this one' remains the best compliment it has received.

List of Abbreviations

Deleuze's works will be referenced using the following abbreviations. The bibliography contains detailed information on the editions used. In the case of the *Abécédaire*, the reference is to the letter which heads the section of the interview: 'C as in *culture*', 'G as in *gauche*', and so on.

A	*L'abécédaire de Gilles Deleuze*
AO	*Anti-Oedipus*
B	*Bergsonism*
C1	*Cinema 1: The Movement-Image*
CC	*Coldness and Cruelty*
D	*Dialogues II*
DR	*Difference and Repetition*
DRM	*Two Regimes of Madness*
DW	'Description of Woman'
ECC	*Essays Critical and Clinical*
PS	*Expressionism in Philosophy: Spinoza*
ES	*Empiricism and Subjectivity*
F	*Foucault*
FLB	*The Fold: Leibniz and the Baroque*
K	*Kafka*
LS	*Logic of Sense*
N	*Negotiations*
NP	*Nietzsche and Philosophy*
PS	*Proust and Signs*

My ideal, when I write about an author, would be to write nothing that could cause him sadness, or if he is dead, that might make him weep in his grave. Think of the author you are writing about. Think of him so hard that he can no longer be an object, and equally so that you cannot identify with him. Avoid the double shame of the scholar and the familiar. Give back to an author a little of the joy, the energy, the political life and the life of love he knew how to give and invent.

Deleuze, *Dialogues*

Introduction

1 Philosophy   The present work is an exposition of the main articulations that constitute Gilles Deleuze's philosophy of law. While far from obvious, there is in fact a complete system of a philosophy of law in Deleuze's works. This system presents itself as rigorously unfolding the consequences implied by *two theses*. The *first* thesis constitutes the system's critical component and can be found in *Coldness and Cruelty*, originally a preface to an edition of *Venus in Furs* by Sacher-Masoch. It is articulated as follows: 'There has only ever been one way of thinking the Law, namely a comic of thinking made up of irony and humor' (*CC*, 86 [modified]). The *second* thesis, which makes up the clinical component of the system, can be found in a conversation with Raymond Bellour and François Ewald included in *Negotiations* under the title 'On Philosophy'. It is articulated as follows: 'Jurisprudence is the philosophy of law, and deals with singularities, it advances by working out from singularities' (*N*, 153). That the totality of Deleuze's system of a philosophy of law is contained in these two theses – and in them alone – is easily explained. Contrary to the domain of the sciences, of cinema, or of marketing, law is echoed in no other way in Deleuze's work than in what follows from these theses. That is to say, the system of philosophy of law Deleuze elaborates is characterised above all by its autonomy, its *autism*, even. Expressing nothing but its own unfolding, law, contrary to the sciences, cinema, or marketing, marks the existence of a boundary shared by the domain reserved for law and that reserved for philosophy. There is a philosophy of law by Deleuze because law is given no place in his philosophy.

2 *Law*   In a conversation with Elie During, Patrice Blouin and Dork Zabunyan, Jacques Rancière once claimed that there is no philosophy of cinema in Deleuze. He states:

> I don't think philosophy is ever *of* this or that. Rather, philosophy is always a discourse *between* one thing and another . . . I am not at all convinced, for example that we find any such thing [as a philosophy of cinema] in Deleuze. He develops a theory of the movement-image and of the time-image. What he proposes, in fact, is a metaphysics that passes through cinema.[1]

In confronting cinema, painting or literature, Deleuze always comes back to philosophy: philosophy is the only addressee of his various efforts. That cinema, the sciences or even politics can learn from these efforts is not a concern that drives him. Why would it be different for law? Because there is, in Deleuze, something prior to his entering into philosophy, a pre-philosophical decision from which his entire philosophy would result. Deleuze articulates this decision in a conversation with Claire Parnet that was filmed and included in the *Abécédaire*. Speaking of the 'left' and of human rights, Deleuze confides that 'I have always been fascinated by jurisprudence, by law. If I hadn't done philosophy, I would have done law' (*A*, G).[2] Going into philosophy, for Deleuze, requires the negative choice of moving away from law, as if law were inaccessible to the efforts of philosophy – as if law testified to the existence of a *prohibition to enter* that philosophy must obey. A little like for Jacques Derrida, for whom law embodied the end of deconstruction, law for Deleuze marks the *terminus ad quem* of philosophy.[3]

3 *Problem*   We may hypothesise that this prohibition never satisfied Deleuze. If it had, the existence, however sparse, of a system of philosophy of law in his work would have to be read as an attempt to go beyond its very terms. Instead of considering the domain of law as closed off from philosophy by an impenetrable border, Deleuze would have tried to articulate the philosophy of law in the terms of philosophy.

2

The genuinely philosophical problem to which the existence of a system of philosophy of law in Deleuze would testify would thus resemble the conflict of the faculties in which Kant intervened. In publishing his eponymous book, Kant intended to make a decisive contribution to settling the conflict that opposed the law faculty and the philosophical faculty, both of which tried to achieve supremacy in the academy in the wake of the ruin of the theological faculty.[4] Deleuze's elaboration of a system of philosophy of law can also be understood as his desire to refuse the determination of the limits of philosophy by anything other than philosophy. That the necessary choice between law and philosophy does not belong to philosophy is something that can and must be fought philosophically: that would be Deleuze's Kantianism. If confirmed, this would imply that his philosophy of law is, in reality, quite the opposite: an anti-philosophy of law – or, at the very least, an anti-juridical philosophy. That, however, would equally mean that the philosophy at issue must be questioned as well. In taking up once more, within the domain of philosophy, the problem of defining the boundary between philosophy and law, it is philosophy that finds itself *declined* (in the grammatical sense). There would no longer be a single philosophy: there would be several.

4 *Alternative*   The problem that haunts Deleuze's philosophy of law is the problem of the becoming of philosophy as such. Should it adopt the *critical* horizon of a thinking of the Law or take the *clinical* path of a pragmatics of judgement? That is the alternative with which readers of Deleuze find themselves confronted the moment they discover the two theses that claim to say all there is to say about law. Nonetheless, Deleuze himself proposes a settlement for this alternative. His proposal takes the following form: only on condition of a critique of the thinking of the Law does a clinic of the practice of law become possible. Among the two forms of philosophy incited by the irruption of law in the field of the preoccupations of thinking, one is the pre-condition of

the other. However, this condition for its part suffers from a weakness: if critique renders a form of clinic possible, it is only insofar as the clinic comes in after the failure of critique. That is to say, in Deleuze's view, critique always stops halfway and everything still remains to be done afterwards – it stops halfway, and that means *nowhere*. But this is foreseeable: in the critical component of his philosophy, the last word has been granted the Law – and this last word, precisely, is what is to be taken away from it. In the clinical component, meanwhile, in order to be able to give law something like dignity, the issue is to restore the first word to philosophy itself, to give it supremacy once more in the thinking of that which concerns it. Deleuze thus deals with the multiplication of possible philosophies by ultimately affirming the unity of philosophy. Taking something like a philosophy of law seriously means taking a detour, the better to return to philosophy as such afterwards. Thus, it is also, for Deleuze, a way of dealing with the existential scruple he revealed to Parnet in a form that does not suffer from regret, for in doing philosophy, Deleuze basically never stopped doing law, that is to say, jurisprudence.

5 Literalness Once Deleuze's system of philosophy of law finds itself subordinate to the rest of his philosophical system, the principles of the latter also apply to the former. Among these, the most important is probably the principle of *literalness* that François Zourabichvili, especially, has shed light on.[5] As Deleuze himself insists on a number of occasions, a philosophical utterance must be read literally, that is to say, without ever being considered the metaphor of anything else.[6] Put differently, behind the apparent sense, behind the surface of an utterance, there is never anything but a bottomless void in which no supplement of sense whatsoever is hiding. The two theses that compose Deleuze's system of philosophy of law, too – the critical thesis and the clinical thesis – must thus be taken literally: if, in fact, there is a thinking of the Law, it cannot but take a comical form, and jurisprudence, in fact, is the philosophy of law. The point is not to read these theses as provocations or jokes but as declarations of a downright ontological nature: they must be read as 'Law = comic' and 'jurisprudence = philosophy'. The principle of literalness allows us to take these two equations seriously, which in Deleuze leave no remainder. The point is to see what these two theses, these two utterances, these two formulas produce rather than to subject them to a pointless semiological critique. In just the same way as Deleuze reads the declarations of the greatest writers as so many *true* propositions, the principle of literalness he applies demands that we read his own propositions with the certainty, maintained throughout, that they, too, are true from beginning to end.

6 Betrayal The principle of literalness Deleuze articulates is nonetheless modelled in a very specific way. In the 'Letter to a Harsh Critic' he addresses to Michel Cressole, he reveals that his practice of the principle of literalness is not without ulterior motives. Beginning his career with systematically confronting the great philosophers who shaped him, he decides to submit to a different principle, a principle of *betrayal*:

> the main way I coped with it at the time was to see the history of philosophy as a sort of buggery or (it comes to the same thing) immaculate conception. I saw myself as taking an author from behind and giving him a child that would be his own offspring, yet monstrous.

Deleuze seeks to make the philosophers he is reading produce something completely different from what they thought they had produced, and to do so with their help. There is, however, an exception to this principle: this exception is Nietzsche. Concerning Nietzsche, Deleuze is compelled to note that 'you just can't deal with him in the same sort of way. He gets up to all sorts of things behind *your* back' (*N*, 6). But perhaps we can apply this ambiguity of the principle of betrayal to the work of Deleuze himself. In a way, the present work is an attempt to get up to something behind Deleuze's back, for the philosophy of law at issue exists in his work only in a state of ruin. And, in a different manner, it also constitutes a way for Deleuze to make me give birth to a philosophy of law that, all things considered, I would never have dared entertain if he had not led me there himself. It's not the least of ironies that in Deleuze, somehow, something of Socrates, that traitor, that pervert, survives.

Notes

1. Rancière, 'The Indecisive Affect', 205 and 206, Rancière's emphases.
2. See also François Dosse's commentary in *Gilles Deleuze and Félix Guattari*, 113–14.
3. See Derrida, 'Force of Law', 15: law 'makes deconstruction possible'.
4. See Kant, *The Conflict of the Faculties*.
5. See Zourabichvili, *The Vocabulary of Deleuze*, 139–42.
6. See the references in Zourabichvili, *The Vocabulary of Deleuze*, 139–42 and note.

I

Critique

1 Thesis I   The first component of Deleuze's philosophy of law is a negative component. It is enounced in the thesis, 'There has only ever been one way of thinking the Law, namely a comic of thinking made up of irony and humor' (CC, 86 [modified]). Deleuze articulates it in his introduction to a translation of Leopold Sacher-Masoch's *Venus in Furs*, which Éditions de Minuit published in 1967 as a complement to the figure of Sade then en vogue. Indeed, Deleuze's entire text, which resembles a work of literary criticism, seeks to establish the difference between sadism and masochism by systematically confronting the two authors' writings. This confrontation takes up subjects as diverse as the authors' relation to language, to description, but also to the Law. The sixth and seventh sections of *Coldness and Cruelty* in particular elaborate on Sade's thinking of the Law insofar as it opposes that of Sacher-Masoch (CC, 69–90). This is where Gilles Deleuze articulates the thesis just quoted; he subsequently develops it by recalling the different strategies with which thinking has sought to deal with it. There is, prior to Sade and Sacher-Masoch, an entire history of the relation to the Law, and the sediments of this history can now be captured in a corpus of thinking. The articulations of this history constitute the negative component of Deleuze's philosophy of law: his complete cartography, as we will see, brings together the entirety of possible relations of thinking to the Law. It is not only an analytical history but indeed a speculative one, and it is a closed history: with Sade, Sacher-Masoch and a few others, both the thinking of the Law and the critique of this thinking have come to an end.

2 Taxonomy   According to Deleuze's thesis, we must posit the Law to be unthinkable otherwise than as comic. This can also be put as: there is no Law other than comic. This comic, meanwhile, can vary considerably. Deleuze operates with *two distinctions* to account for these variations: (a) there is always, first, a distinction between *image* of thought and *critique* of thought in matters of the Law; and (b) there is a distinction between the *classical* and the *modern* relation to the Law. When these two distinctions are combined, there are *four modes* in which the Law can be comic: (a) classical image; (b) classical critique; (c) modern image; and (d) modern critique. There are *four figures*, Deleuze goes on to say, that can be associated with these four modes of being and that express their essence: (a) Plato for the classical image; (b) Socrates's students for classical critique; (c) Kant for the modern image; and (d) a curious constellation encompassing, at a minimum, Sade and Sacher-Masoch for the modern critique. The aim of the sixth and seventh sections of *Coldness and Cruelty* is to elucidate this complex taxonomy of relations to the Law. However, this elucidation, too, finds itself dependent on the principle of comprehension articulated by the thesis: all the branches of the taxonomy belong to the comic genre. Both the image that thinking has of the Law and its critique, both the classic and the modern, must be understood as so many manifestations of the comic. And, moreover, these different manifestations spell themselves out, according to their movement, as *irony* and *humour*. This multiplies the number of branches included in the taxonomy by two, bringing them to eight, even if the distinction between irony and humour seems

	CLASSICAL	MODERN
THINKING	Plato	Kant
CRITIQUE	Socrates's disciples	*Irony*: Sade
		Humour: Sacher-Masoch

Figure 1 Taxonomy of the relations of thinking to the Law

8

really to concern only the different forms of the critique of the thinking of the Law.

3 Plato   The *first* figure in the history of the thinking of the Law that interests Deleuze is Plato. It is he who has the dubious honour of having given 'perfect expression' to the classical image of the Law, an expression that later 'gained universal acceptance throughout the Christian world'.[1] This image, Deleuze goes on to say, breaks up into *two points of view*: the point of view of principles and that of consequences. (a) From the point of view of principles, 'the law itself is not a primary but only a secondary or delegated power dependent on a supreme principle which is the Good'. (b) From the point of view of consequences, this implies that obedience to the Law can be considered what is best, 'the best being in the image of the Good'. This breaking up, which constitutes the operation by which Plato establishes the classical image of the Law, evidently consists in a relationship of dependence between the Law and *two levels* that exceed it: (a) the Good, considered superior to the Law; and (b) the Best, whereby determining the Best allows for judging the Law by the measure of the Good. The classical image of the Law thus takes an asymmetrical shape: the Best is determined in the name of the Good, and the Law is judged in the name of the Best. For Deleuze, this is the matrix of a dual comic. 'There is indeed a great deal of irony in the operation that seeks to trace the laws back to an absolute Good as the necessary principle of their foundation', he writes. 'Equally, there is considerable humour in the attempt to reduce the laws to a relative Best in order to persuade us that we should obey them.' The Law needs the crutches of the Good and the Best to function because it is not functioning and has no chance whatsoever to function, be it with or without these crutches.

4 Socrates   Nothing reveals the dual comic character of this classical image of the Law better than Plato's own presentation of Socrates's trial in the *Apology*. While the speeches of

Socrates himself seem to manifest a perfectly serious spirit, his disciples, for their part, draw from them the most profound conclusions: that in fact all of this is comic. It is ironic, first of all, to find oneself condemned by a Law supposed to emanate from the Good when Socrates is himself asked to accept this condemnation. And it is humorous to choose to die for a Law of which one knows very well that the Best expected from it turns out at best to be illusory, at worst to be something worse, an injustice. In consequence, Socrates's disciples at the moment of his condemnation could not have found anything better to do than to burst into laughter, in keeping with Socrates's own advice. The laughter of Socrates's disciples appears to Deleuze as the manifestation of a critique of the classical image of the Law, as a critique immanent to this image (CC, 82). Not only does this image prove to be comic in itself, this comic character can manifest in a form that both reveals and highlights it. In other words, it is perfectly possible to imagine that the comic of this classical image of the Law does not appear: out of conviction, out of stupidity, or out of interest. But this possibility is in itself a doubling of the comic in that it is the most profound manifestation of the comic: that the comic character of the Law does not appear does, in itself, manifest this comic character even more than if it appeared in the light of day. This explains the disciples' gratuitous laughter, a laughter devoid of all reproach and all bitterness: in fact, the joke has been kept up all the way to the end, that is to say, until its fall, which corresponds to the fall of Socrates himself.

5 Kant I   Deleuze explains that Kant, having destroyed the classical image of the Law, replaces it, and its critique, with something like a modern image. His destruction of the old image has *two aspects*: a reversal of the relationship of the Law to the Good and a reversal of its relationship with the Best. With the first reversal, Kant seeks to make it such that, in order for it to be possible to say that the law is founded, the Law no longer needs any higher authority. If it must be founded, Kant claims in the Second Critique, it cannot be founded otherwise than on itself, that is to say, on that which constitutes its specificity as Law: the form of the Law. Because the Law is a Law and because it thus satisfies the formal conditions that make it a Law (which are articulated in conformity with the demands of Kant's ethics), it can be said to be founded.

> Whereas the classical conception only dealt with *the laws* according to the various spheres of the Good or the various circumstances attending the Best, Kant can speak of the moral law, and of its application to what otherwise remains totally undetermined. The moral law is the representation of a pure form and is independent of content or object, spheres of activity or circumstances. The moral law is THE LAW, the form of the law and as such it cannot be grounded in a higher principle (CC, 82–3, Deleuze's emphasis).

Against the Platonic image of the Law that had the Law revolve around the Good, Kant's Copernican Revolution consists in making the Good revolve around the Law. In doing so, Kant marks the end of the Christian age nourished by the Platonic image and also, perhaps, the end of a pre-Christian, Judaic, even pre-Socratic age in which the main characteristic of the object of the Law was essentially to unveil itself (CC, 83).

6 Kant II Just as Kant reversed the dependence of the Law on the Good established by Plato, he also reversed the dependence of the Law on the Best as the marker of its merits: 'the Best as representing the good will of the righteous' can no longer serve to sanction the Law. Once the Law is without both content and object, that is, once it finds itself summed up in its form of Law, the circumstances of its action lose all importance. As Deleuze says,

> THE LAW, as defined by its pure form, without substance or object or any determination whatsoever, is such that no one knows nor can know what it is. It operates without making itself known. It

defines a realm of transgression where one is already guilty, and where one oversteps the bounds without knowing what they are. (CC, 83–4)

Henceforth, neither the Best nor the Worst is possible anymore: all there is is a state in which the Law can be said to conform or not to conform to its form of Law or, put differently, to conform or not to conform to the only possible Good of which it is the embodiment.

> If the law is no longer based on the Good as a preexisting, higher principle, and it is valid by virtue of its form alone, the content remaining entirely undetermined, it becomes impossible to say that the righteous man obeys the law for the sake of the Best. In other words, the man who obeys the law does not thereby become righteous or feel righteous; on the contrary, he feels guilty and is guilty in advance, and the more strict his obedience, the greater his guilt. (CC, 84)

The Platonic logic of the possible redemption of those who follow the Law is replaced with a paradoxical logic: the purer the Law, the guiltier we are; the more we follow the Law, the more all possibility of redemption eludes us. This amounts to saying that, properly speaking, *there is no justice anymore*: once the Best, which it was the wise man's task to determine (since the wise man is the one who knows the Good), finds itself merged with the simple existence of the Law, the possibility too of a justice understood as this excess of the Best over a given state is abolished.

7 Freud   Kant's double reversal of the classical image of the Law elaborated by Plato contains a *double paradox*, which is the source of its comic character. According to Deleuze, Freud gives expression to this paradox in his theory of moral conscience in *Civilization and its Discontents*. For Freud, moral conscience is in fact doubly paradoxical. (a) The first paradox is that 'the renunciation of instinctual gratification is not the product of conscience, but on the contrary that conscience itself is born of such renunciation'. (b) Similarly, the second paradox is that 'the law is the same as repressed desire. The law cannot specify its object without self-contradiction, nor can it define itself with reference to a content without removing the repression on which it rests. The object of the law and the object of desire are one and the same, and remain equally concealed' (CC, 84). The modern image of the Law that Kant elaborates can be said to illustrate this double paradox of moral conscience because it inverts the relationship of subordination that placed the stakes of the Law outside the Law. On the one hand, it deprives the Law of any reason it has to exist by turning it into a creation in which what is at stake is itself; but on the other hand, these remaining stakes find themselves cancelled out by the prohibition to articulate themselves. Once the Law merges with the moral desire that haunts it, a desire whose form is expression, the truth of the Law can no longer be articulated without depriving itself of what remained of its reason to exist, that is to say, its form. There is thus indeed a Kantian irony and a Kantian humour: an irony that consists in taking away the founding that one is looking for and a humour that consists in taking away the possibility of affirming this absence of founding. Not only does the Law no longer have crutches to walk on, but, as Sartre saw, it finds itself deprived of the hands that would allow it to grasp them.

8 *Sade I* It is amusing to realise that Kant, more than anyone else, ought to be considered the philosopher of the impossible Law. But the history of the thinking of the Law Deleuze sketches does not stop there. Responding to the modern image of the Law elaborated by Kant is a modern critique which spells out the comic aspects of this image even further. According to Deleuze, the first figure to intervene in the sense of such a critique is Sade, who embodies its ironic side. Yet if, Deleuze notes, irony consists precisely 'in the process or movement which bypasses the law as a merely secondary power and aims at transcending it toward a higher principle', then what happens once this superior principle is

gone (CC, 86)? The response could not be simpler: all it takes is to invent a new one. There is nonetheless one condition for this invention: the new principle at issue is not so much to produce a new foundation of the law than the inverse. Since Kant conceived of an impossible founding of the law, all it takes is to reverse this impossibility and expose the only principle capable of resolving the paradox. According to Sade, this absolutely univocal principle is Evil: not moral Evil but natural Evil, the Evil of a nature of which the Law is never anything but the most actualised expression. The task, therefore, is no longer to reverse the Law (this, Kant claimed for himself) but to overcome it in following a movement from the bottom up that traverses it and that we might qualify as *perversion*. This perversion of the Law consequently perverts second nature, the artificial and tyrannical nature expressed by the Law, into a primary nature that turns tyranny into a paradoxical Good. Sade must be reread as the thinker of the reconciliation of the Law with nature – and thus of the Law with its own formal requirements: only in Sade is Kant's formalism really sustainable.

9 Sade II Corresponding to the ascending movement of irony is the vertical overcoming of the law: that is the sense of perversion. The scope of this perversion is immense because it proceeds to buy out or redeem the Kantian paradox. As Deleuze explains, '[i]t follows that the idea of absolute evil embodied in primary nature', which Sade pursued, 'cannot be equated either with tyranny – for tyranny still presupposes laws – or with a combination of whims and arbitrariness; its higher, impersonal model is rather to be found in the anarchic institutions of perpetual motion and permanent revolution. Sade often stresses the fact that the law can only be transcended toward an institutional model of anarchy' (CC, 87). The annulment of the Law sought by Kant actualises, according to Sade, in an *institution* that has no need of the Law. That this institution is temporary does not matter to him at all: the institution is a moment, a blessed *kairos*, an event, in which the abolition of all Law is finally justified. This is Sade's anxious side: he could not bear the abyss with which Kant's thinking of the Law confronts us. And it is also his logician's side: the paradoxes of the modern image of the Law must be replaced with some kind of consistency. In actualising the overcoming of the Law, an institution such as the Society of the Friends of Crime does not expose the hypocrisy of the Law – that is the banality Socrates's disciples were laughing at – but on the contrary its fantastic lack of hypocrisy. By taking recourse to the principle of Evil, Sade affirms not only the univocity of this principle, of primary nature, but also the univocity of the Law itself, a Law that is not only without founding but bottomless. A 'de-founded' (foundered) Law, a pure simulacrum, a mask of nothing, yet a 'foundering' from above, through the roof, as it were, as if the Law were a door open to the stars. Solar anus.

10 Ost   We might even go further in identifying the figure of Sade with that of Kant. If Deleuze is right, and if Sade does indeed actualise the virtualities at work in Kant's thinking, then we would have to go as far as identifying, as François Ost has done, Sade with Portalis, the principal author of the Napoleonic *Code civil*. In the final dialogue of his *Sade et la loi*, Ost in fact imagines the confrontation between the two some night in 1793: a fierce but polite dialogue from which both apparently emerge intact.[2] Yet we might surmise that this is just for show: the confrontation takes place because, basically, Portalis and Sade are one and the same person. Why? Because the *Code civil* is born from the anarchical institution of the Terror – just as, in Sade, the statutes of the Society of the Friends of Crime emerge once the Society has been founded, a little like its epitaph. The paradox of the *Code* is that, as its tombstone, it is the greatest monument ever erected in honour of the Terror, the Terror that called for a legal codex and made it possible. The Terror is that event without Law in which primary nature expresses itself par excellence, and it was only logical that it would give rise to a codex that would proclaim its definitive completion. Rather than consider the *Code civil* as that which would protect us from a possible return to the Terror, we ought to see it as the last active trace, the last living spark of the Terror. And Portalis, whose entire life can be summarised as the gestation and labour of this *Code*, his most famous child, is perhaps also the most important figure of the Terror. Not Robespierre, who never stopped looking for new, ever more paradoxical justifications for his actions (Robespierre was, basically, a Kantian), but Sade: that is the reversal to which the *Code civil* testifies to this day. The *Code civil* is the product of the perversion of the Law, the melancholic trace of its impossibility.

11 Sacher-Masoch I   If Sade embodies the ironic aspect of the critique of the Kantian image of the Law, then Sacher-Masoch, according to Deleuze, embodies the humorous aspect. Just as Sade sought to operate the overcoming of the Law by taking recourse to a higher institution, so Sacher-Masoch operates the circumvention of the Law by scrupulously applying the Law. There is a masochist art of consequences that consists in taking the Law literally and in submitting to it without regard to any other consideration whatsoever. 'By observing the very letter of the law, we refrain from questioning its ultimate or primary character; we then behave as if the supreme sovereignty of the law conferred upon it the enjoyment of all those pleasures that it denies us . . . A close examination of masochistic fantasies or rites reveals that while they bring into play the very strictest application of the law, the result in every case is the opposite of what might be expected' (CC, 88). The masochistic circumvention of the Law can be said to be humorous in that it considers the Law as if the paradox of its application (recalled by Freud) was of no importance, or rather as if this paradox, far from placing the Law in a position of impossibility, was what allowed for the full and complete *jouissance* of the Law. To have *jouissance* of the Law is thus, as it is for Sade, to trust the image of the Law defined by

Kant to such a degree that the image is redeemed by its sins. Where Kant admitted his inability to make the paradox live-able (the paradox consists in the Law's respect for its form of Law being the source of a general culpabilisation), masochist humour manages to *positivise* the culpabilisation the Law entails. It does not matter what fault we committed, it does not matter even whether we committed any at all, *as long as the Law claims the opposite*. In fact, there is no masochistic *jouissance* except in a Kantian context: a formal context in which punishment pre-exists all fault, a punishment whose application is, precisely, the *subversion* of the Law.

12 Sacher-Masoch II   Yet just like Sade's ironic perversion, the humorous subversion of the modern image of the Law that Sacher-Masoch operates is not without concomitants. The impossible character of this image in fact requires restoring an exteriority that allows for marshalling it against itself. Kant – close to Leibniz in this regard – wanted to see in the Law an authority susceptible to a founding of its own, almost an autistic founding: both Sade and Sacher-Masoch open the doors and windows once more. But where Sade sought to overcome the Law with the help of an institution that rises above it, Sacher-Masoch seeks to bypass it via an author-ity that depends on the Law. Because masochist humour is an art of consequences, this authority is the *contract*, the very contract of which the Law (article 2279 of the *Code civil*) says that it counts as Law for those who enter into it. There is a full-fledged masochist theory of the contract, to which Deleuze dedicates an entire section, the eighth section of *Coldness and Cruelty*. In substance, this theory aims to operate a kind of fusion of natural contract and private con-tract: when a masochist signs a contract with a mistress, the goal is to overwhelm the Law with the assistance of the Law: 'he suggests that contracts should be drawn up with a terrible Tsarina, thus ensuring the most sentimental but at the same time the coldest and severest law' (CC, 93). Just how far can the application of the Law go? And just how far can the implication of the Law go? Contents to be applied and measures to apply them can be infinite provided they obey the formal definition of the Law. The Law loses all moral pertinence. From the moral point of view it is a mad Law, but this madness is the madness of the moral point of view itself! Like Sade, Sacher-Masoch sees himself above all as the most logical of Kantians – the only difference is his Zen attitude, which contrasts with Sade's anxiety.

13 Lacan In his famous article, 'Kant with Sade', Jacques Lacan brings out this profound complicity between the work of Sade and the ideas of Kant. According to Lacan, Sade's oeuvre constitutes the reverse of what Kant's oeuvre is the obverse of: the place where the libidinal real of the moral Law – which itself is the imaginary expression of the symbolic LAW – expresses itself. But perhaps he should have said the same thing about Sacher-Masoch's oeuvre. Even more so than Sade, Sacher-Masoch takes the Kantian moral Law seriously: he goes so far as to accept it unconditionally, to put everything into motion to extend it to the maximum. Sade is concerned with inventing a new foundation that serves to smash the moral Law, to obliterate it, or turn it into a blow-up doll. Sacher-Masoch, by contrast, never attempts to turn the Law into anything other than what it is. In his eyes, the Law affirms strictly nothing: it is nothing but the occasion of witnessing, in the fall of the moral Law, the fall of the great symbolic LAW that was still there in Sade. In this sense, Deleuze operates the critique of Lacanian psychoanalysis, to which he would later devote some effort, already in *Coldness and Cruelty*. To establish the equation *Sade = Kant* means still to trust too much in the hypothesis of a LAW that would undergird the nullity of all Laws: a form of the form of Law, itself empty, like Lacan's great Other. To establish the equation *Sacher-Masoch = Kant*, on the contrary, amounts to saying that if in the Kantian as in the Sadean construct, the form of Law is without hope, then this absence of hope must also apply to everything that could redeem it. At the same time, this also results in de-dramatising Sade, in turning one's perversion into something so univocal, so un-Bataillian, as Sacher-Masoch's subversion.

14 Kant III   Kant's humour and irony must be understood as different from Sacher-Masoch's humour and Sade's irony. This difference may be qualified as follows. Where the humour and irony manifested by Socrates's disciples expressed, in a singular mode, what already belonged to the Platonic comic itself, the humour manifested by Sacher-Masoch and the irony manifested by Sade for their part bring out something foreign to Kant's humour and irony. There is, in fact, something sad about Kant's humour and irony: unlike Plato, Kant does not seem to notice that he is ridiculous – and in consequence, he does not at all understand the laughter that Sade and Sacher-Masoch address to him. The critique of the classical image of the Law was *immanent*: image and critique shared the same comic. The critique of the modern image of the Law in turn is incommensurable with the Law: the comic of the image benefits from the blindness of the Law. In the case of Kant, we might thus speak of a *transcendental* comic: a comic that, starting from the image of the Law it outlines, escapes the Law and remains invisible to it at the very moment that it explains and even constitutes its essence. This transcendental comic contrasts with the comic immanent to the classical image of the Law of which Plato staged both the establishment and the critique. Perhaps it was Kant's blindness to himself that one day moved Deleuze to pity, which would explain why, despite his repulsion, he devoted an entire book to opening an emergency exit from Kant's own Kantianism. In *Kant's Critical Philosophy*, Deleuze praises the theory of the faculties through which Kant reintroduced proliferation at the core of his ordered philosophy. Deleuze was fully aware, of course, that the key to this theory was the conflict that at that time opposed the philosophical faculty to the law faculty in Germany. To reintroduce proliferation was to save philosophy itself and to vindicate philosophy against the Law. Perhaps Kant was not that blind after all.

15 Irony   What is irony? In *Coldness and Cruelty*, Deleuze gives a definition that is a little too short: irony is an ascending movement towards an impossible founding. In *Logic of Sense*, he comes back to the concept and to its difference from humour (and, incidentally, from satire). He even devotes a full series to them, the nineteenth, entitled 'Of Humor' (*LS*, 134–41). What does he say there? First of all, as in the earlier text, there are different forms of irony: just as there is a history of the thinking of the Law in which irony intervenes, so there is a history of irony as such. Deleuze distinguishes between *three forms* of irony: there is, first, Socratic irony, then classical irony, and then Romantic irony. *Socratic* irony may be described as 'a matter of disentangling, from a combined threefold operation, a universal form of the individual (reality), and, at the same time, of extracting a pure Idea of what we speak about (necessity), and of confronting language with an ideal model assumed to be primitive, natural, or purely rational (possibility)'. The issue is to mark a difference between the Idea and the individual who has an idea and to define this difference as proceeding to operate the subsumption of the individual under the Idea. 'It is precisely this conception which animates Socratic irony as an ascent, and gives it at once the following tasks: to tear the individual away from his or her immediate existence; to transcend sensible particularity towards the Idea; and to establish laws of language corresponding to the model' (*LS*, 137–8). Irony is the expression of a desire to *rectify* what appears as a deficit in the register of the individual – a deficit, however, that will always remain active since only the disappearance of the individual in the Idea would be able to actualise the rectification. This, according to Deleuze, is the farcical aspect that remains a driving force all the way to the dialogue between Socrates and Alcibiades in the *Symposium*: the solution is only a metaphor.

16 Irony II   Classical irony (which corresponds to the era of the modern image of the Law) and Romantic irony present themselves as two ways of suturing the wound inflicted by Socratic irony. *Classical* irony operates this suture by means of representation, where Being and individual join and become one – unless the representation is an image. *Romantic* irony, in turn, operates the suture by transforming this image into a simulacrum: the representation that unifies Being and individual must now correspond to the I of the person who conceives of it. 'The position of the person as an unlimited class, which nevertheless has only one member (I) – such is the Romantic irony' (*LS*, 139). In classical irony, we easily recognise the attempt, actualised by Kant, of providing the finitude of the human being with a metaphysical foundation: we must accept that the conjunction of individual and Idea jokingly suggested by Socrates is impossible. It is an irony because, as we saw concerning the moral Law, this act implies a form of reconciliation, itself impossible, of the individual with its finite nature. Romanticism refuses such reconciliation when it makes irreconcilability the source of its irony: a black irony in which despair teams up with cosmic megalomania. The person will never reconcile with Being, nor for that matter with the Idea, but this is precisely what allows it access to the torn heart of things, to their painfully incomplete Being. For Deleuze, however, in all three cases there is something like a Ground speaking behind these proclamations of rupture: the ground of the Idea, of Being, or of the senseless universe. Two years after *Coldness and Cruelty*, irony becomes itself a problem: its foundering was not real. At bottom, irony is a melancholy of the image it claims to pervert.

17 Humour I   Perhaps the nostalgia of a ground that haunts irony ought to be replaced with humour as an 'art of surfaces': the perversion of causes is followed by a subversion. Yet there is a strange lack of rigour on Deleuze's part here: he speaks of Sade's perversion, but he also evokes the perversion constituted by the 'art of surfaces' (*LS*, 133).[3] Perhaps this is because there is more than just irony in Sade's perversion: Sade's critique of Kant's image of the Law is ironic towards the irony embodied by this very image. Could there be something like an ironic humour? This would make everything very complicated. Yet what is humour? In a first approximation, we might say that it is a descending movement, made up of non-sense and speed (*LS*, 135–6). Where irony consists in always operating the movement up towards an eternal principle capable of yielding a signification (a depth, a ground) to what it governs, humour consists in letting oneself go down a surface without any other signification (without any other thickness, any other ground) than the ever faster multiplication of consequences it entails. But the notion of a descent must not be seen as a metaphor that would imply a form of laisser-faire, of fatalism, or of approval for what it is leading towards: the characteristic of the humorous descent, on the contrary, is that it has no destination. It is a pure movement whose very trajectory traces the surface of apparition of something like an event, an event which proves to be as devoid of sense as the surface and the movement that constitute the coordinates of its apparition. Humour is thus no more a method than it is a system: it is another name for the attitude of the one who is ready to welcome an event in all the gratuitousness of its non-sense.

18 Humour II Surfaces and consequences versus ground and causes – perhaps Deleuze should have inverted the lexicon here: there is a subversive dimension to irony that is due to the possibility that it give rise to a humorous event. But it is not possible for ironic perversion to become a humorous procedure without humour losing what constitutes its force, namely its connection with non-sense. We can pervert sense with the help of something else but perverting it still consists in working with it, whereas subverting sense aims at discarding it forever, at opening oneself to non-sense. In this regard, we may say that Deleuze's theory of humour is a theory that aims to describe the existing effective spectrum of differences between humour and irony. Irony is weaker than humour because it continues to refer to a principle, however devoid of signification that principle may be. Humour, inversely, because it needs neither tools nor supports, proves to be endowed with the full force of those for whom what's important is always elsewhere. There is a profound idiocy on the part of humour, whose privileged embodiment in Deleuze is Dostoevsky's Prince Myshkin. Confronted with the necessity to seek help in order to save the one he loves, Myshkin keeps letting himself be distracted by other things along the way. Yet these distractions are not so many traps laid along his path: at the moment he encounters them, they become more important than what, *in principle*, would exclusively claim all his attention. The same applies to the masochist: the contract to which he submits is the meticulous protocol of the elaboration of a *jouissance* whose importance always makes him yield to the events to which the contract gives rise. In masochism, *jouissance* is a deception: the only thing that counts is the scrupulous fulfilment of the clauses that the contract manages to extort from the Law as so many manifestations of its non-sense.

19 Satire   In *Logic of Sense*, Deleuze presents a third form of the comic that he does not develop in *Coldness and Cruelty*. This third form is satire. Unlike irony and humour, satire does not benefit from any special philosophical attention on Deleuze's part. On the last pages of the thirty-fourth series, he is content with having it appear as an almost archaic figure: 'Satire is a prodigious art of regressions', it is the art of returning 'bottomless depth' (the surfaces) and 'unlimited height' (the principles) to the chaos they share. Embodied by insults and obscenities, satire in a way testifies to a lost world: the world where differentiating between irony and humour is not yet possible. That may be why Deleuze contents himself with referring the satiric position to that of 'the great pre-Socratic', who, in 'one and the same movement of the world, pursues God with insults and sinks into the excrement' (*LS*,

246). Satire is the comic characteristic of a world in which principles and consequences, depths and surfaces are not yet distinct. It might therefore not be mentioned in *Coldness and Cruelty* because the Law is the phenomenon par excellence born from this distinction. Something like the Law is invented because the depths must be distinguished from the surface, the principles from the consequences. The Law is the means by which verticality and horizontality articulate themselves: it provides the abscissa and the ordinate of the world, if you like. Where there is nothing but chaos, no Law exists: this is so banal that all satire about it is really talking about nothing at all, which is why such satire is so common and so fickle.

20 Kafka I   It seems that the history of the thinking of the Law Deleuze sketches in *Coldness and Cruelty* does not stop with irony and humour. He also evokes, placing him in parallel with Socrates's disciples, the figure of Kafka: like the disciples, Kafka establishes a relationship with the Law marked by laughter. In several places, however, Deleuze seems to consider Kafka an embodiment of a modern form of humour as well, all in all in the same way as Sacher-Masoch (*CC*, 85–6).[4] But maybe we should differentiate between the two. Their difference lies not in the relation to the Law but in the medium of this relation. Both are concerned with deploying an art of consequences in relation to the modern image of the Law, a relation to the Best that it is supposed to produce by itself. Yet where Sacher-Masoch is concerned with subverting this image through recourse to a contract that respects it too much, Kafka is concerned with something entirely different from drawing the undesirable consequences from the Law. Kafka seeks to show how, as such, the most natural consequences of the Law are comical, to expose the Kantian paradox of consequences in those circumstances that are closest to the ordinary. In the fifth chapter of the book on Kafka he co-wrote with Félix Guattari, Deleuze thus presents Kafka as the author of the best *description* of Kant's thinking of the Law. This description addresses the *three aspects* of this thinking that are the most important: (a) its a priori character; (b) its unknowable character; and (c) its character as utterance (*K*, 44–5). You'll recall that characteristically, Kant's image of the Law not only has as its only goal the production of guilty persons, it also has no other conceivable reason to exist than the formal necessity of the punishment whose pronouncement it allows for.

21 Kafka II The three characteristic traits of the modern image of the Law thus all pertain to an idea of necessity: 'From the point of view of a supposed transcendence of the law, there must be a certain necessary connection of the law with guilt, with the unknowable, with the sentence or the utterance' (*K*, 44). Yet, as Deleuze and Guattari note, Kafka's *Trial* offers a meticulous '*dismantling* (*démontage*) and even . . . demolition, throughout K.'s long experimentation' (*K*, 45, Deleuze and Guattari's emphasis [modified]). What are the stages of this dismantling? The first stage is to eliminate any notion of culpability a priori: 'culpability is never anything but the superficial movement whereby judges and even lawyers confine you in order to prevent you from engaging in a real movement – that is, from taking care of your own affairs' (*K*, 45). Rather than as instituting an a priori culpability, the modern image of the Law must be described as establishing an a priori innocence, an innocence that is known to everyone (and especially lawyers and judges) and for that reason is always denied. In Kafka, there is the very opposite of a pathos of the Law: the paradox of consequences in Kant here finds itself taken down in its very description and built up as something else that is no longer pathetic but comic. The culpability at issue in Kafka's texts (letters, novellas, and novels) is a consequence of the functioning of the assemblage in which the Law participates: in itself, as Kant guessed, this culpability is nothing but a paradox. What Kafka does is add a note to Kant that consists in operating the literal description of what in Kant exists only as an anxiety or suspicion. Or, if you prefer, it consists in liberating Kant from his Kantianism by returning the Law to the genius of nullity that Kant refused to grant it, believing as he did that nullity was something to be combatted or at the very least strictly circumscribed.

22 Kafka III   The same goes for the two other aspects of the Law. As far as the necessity of its unknowable character is concerned, Kafka shows that this is not due to its transcendental form but quite simply to the void or desertedness of this form. '[I]f the law remains unrecognizable, this is not because it is hidden by its transcendence, but simply because it is always denuded of any interiority: it is always in the office next door, or behind the door, on to infinity.' It is the assemblage in which the law inscribes itself that proves to bear the impossibility of knowing the Law: no one, in any office, truly knows it or is even in a position to know it one day. Similarly, as far as its character as sentence or utterance is concerned, Kafka shows that

> it is not the law that is stated because of the demands of a hidden transcendence; it is almost the exact opposite: it is the statement, the enunciation, that constructs the law in the name of an immanent power of the one who enounces it – the law is confused with that which the guardian utters, and the writings precede the law, rather than being the necessary and derived expression of it. (*K*, 45)[5]

There is nothing necessary about the Law taking the form of a sentence: it could take any form whatsoever provided the one who enounces it is in some way – and be it completely unfounded – entitled to do so. As was the case for its a priori character, the Law's character as unknowable and as utterance is devoid of the necessity Kant associated with it. What counts in matters of Law is not the form of the Law itself but the contingent form of the assemblage in which it finds itself situated. This is the comic pragmatism that Kafka opposes to Kant's (equally comic) idealism: speaking of the Law as such has *in fact* no signification: signification appears only once the slope it is gliding down is determined, that is to say, once the description that makes the slope exist is completed by the experimentation that drives signification.

23 Kafka IV There is, in Kafka, an entire philosophy of the judicial machinery. This philosophy, however, is deployed entirely from the point of view of the Law. There are *three possible types* of machines: machinic indexes, abstract machines, and assemblages of machines. In Kafka's work, all situations in which the provisional state of a not yet completely assembled machine appears (metamorphosis) correspond to *machinic indexes*. Those situations, in contrast, that appear all at once but without manifesting any functionality (the penal colony) correspond to *abstract machines*. The proliferating figures that keep metamorphosising and thus keep disassembling, which make Kafka's oeuvre stand out, finally, correspond to *assemblages of machines*. It is among these assemblages that Kafka addresses the judicial machinery. What he does with it is describe its threefold movement of proliferation (the Law is everywhere), transformation (everything is the Law), and disassemblage or dismantling (the Law does not hold). This dismantling, however, is not a critique; on the contrary, it is the manifestation of a humour, of an art of consequences. The method of dismantling 'consists . . . of prolonging, of accelerating, a whole movement that already is traversing the social field', that is to say, of making it multiply its own consequences. The law, thus, is a social *practice* on which one claims to ground a *procedure* when at bottom all it expresses is the comic assemblage of the *trial*. This is the very *process* of Kafka's humour, a process of dismantling that works an *inversion*: in the trial, we believed, there was Law when, as we now realise, all there is is desire. As Deleuze and Guattari write: 'the law is written in a porno book' (*K*, 48–9).

24 Kafka V Let's sum up. The modern image of the Law rests on a comic paradox. This paradox is the object of

Kafka's description. This description consists in dismantling the machinery in which the Law is caught up. This dismantling, for its part, merely respects the consequences of what the Law produces: it is the Law itself that dismantles itself. Note, however, that these consequences are absolute: the annulment of the Law itself by the desire that undergirds it. As Deleuze and Guattari write: 'Repression doesn't belong to justice unless it is also desire itself – desire in the one who is repressed as well as in the one who represses' (K, 49). It is this desire that moulds the machinic assemblage of the Law and that opposes it to the Kantian abstract machine, which, for that matter, was undoubtedly moulded by an identical desire of repression. This is Kafka's final lesson: to imagine Kant alone at his desk, foaming at the mouth, in the process of writing the first paragraphs of the *Groundwork of the Metaphysics of Morals*. But there is more than humour here: there is a form of absurdity in the non-sense that might permit speaking of *nonsense* when it comes to Kafka. A bit like the Lewis Carroll of *Logic of Sense*, Kafka takes the consequences as far as they can go without making a single move. The humour of Sacher-Masoch, for his part, implies an inventiveness in betrayal that Kafka does not need: as Deleuze and Guattari acknowledge, Kafka is closer to Carroll than he will ever be to Sacher-Masoch or Sade (K, 93n8). Just as for Carroll, non-sense arises from sense itself, so for Kafka, the inversion of the Law proceeds from the Law itself, namely from the fact that what forms its core is in fact the core of something else. Kafka's great question might be: why would you want to be unfaithful to the Law when being faithful to it is impossible?

25 Cacciari One of the most important theses Deleuze develops concerning Kafka is undoubtedly the assertion that Kafka's oeuvre is not tragic. Contrary to what is often claimed, Kafka's dismantling of the machinic assemblage of the justice apparatus is in fact above all comic in nature. Whether the concern is with its a priori character, its unknowable character, or its character as utterance, this assemblage never takes the bereaved form of an impossibility. It is precisely against this Kantian aspect of the modern image of the Law that Kafka revolts. Yet this strict distinction between comic and tragic has been the object of contestation on the part of Massimo Cacciari. In *Icone della legge* (*Icons of the Law*), he asserts that despite certain comic aspects, Kafka's work must above all be considered tragic.[6] Why? Because the description it gives leads to unearthing the final aporia of the Law, which is that it must be decided. Yet there is no decision, Cacciari explains, that could ever be grounded. That is precisely what Kafka shows: there is a necessity to decide but this necessity provides the decision with no grounding whatsoever. Meanwhile, since deciding always takes place in a void, it is indeed a certain art of consequences that is at issue here: in order gradually to constitute the repercussions of a decision, it is necessary to follow the movement of the void. That is the reason why, when it comes to Kafka, we must speak of tragedy, even if in fact this tragedy is never sad or solemn. It's just that, quite simply, the structure of all decisions is tragic in itself. Nonetheless, for Deleuze, is not such a 'tragedy' precisely what makes Kafka laugh? Is it not precisely that on the subject of which Kafka manifests the most joyful *nonsense*?

26 Bartleby I   There is a Platonism of Kafka's. It consists in reintegrating into the Law what Kant refused to see in it: that it is comic *in itself*. But Kafka is not alone in this. Deleuze brings one more conceptual persona into the critique of the thinking of the Law inaugurated by *Coldness and Cruelty*. This persona does not figure in this first text but appears in others as a sort of double of Kafka, particularly in 'Bartleby; or, The Formula', which featured as postface to a re-edition of Melville's short story.[7] In this text, Deleuze presents Bartleby, the scrivener hired by a Wall Street lawyer to do copying-work, as the quintessential *résistant*. To any request by his employer, Bartleby responds: 'I would prefer not to', leaving the lawyer in perfect suspense. According to

Deleuze, the effectiveness of this formula on those around Bartleby, and particularly on his employer, is explained by the fact that everyone seems to acknowledge its validity in advance. In Melville's story, it is as if there was a *pact* between Bartleby and his employer, a pact stronger than all the labour relations that bind the two men. And each time the lawyer asks Bartleby to perform a certain task, it is as if he breaks that pact, which consists precisely in Bartleby accomplishing *something* without being seen. Yet what the formula pronounced by Bartleby produces is not only the reactivation of this primary pact, it is above all the annihilation of any and all alternatives to this pact: an annihilation that concerns both what is not preferred and what is preferred. What the formula produces, Deleuze says, is 'a negativism beyond all negation' (*ECC*, 71), that is to say, a zone of indiscernibility between the preferable and the non-preferable.

27 Bartleby II   This negativism beyond all negation manifested by Bartleby's repeated formula represents another way the Law has of negating itself, namely to negate itself from the inside. The Law, embodied by the obligations that tie the employee to his employer, finds itself always subordinated to the pact expressed by this formula because this pact, too, embodies this Law. Yet since the Law has more force in the form of a pact than in the form of labour law, the pact wins out over labour law in the very name of the Law. What is comic about 'Bartleby' is that in manifesting the truth of the Law more strongly, the pact that unites the scrivener with his employer ultimately ends in its negation. The pact embodies the pure form of the Law, and this embodiment defeats all other, less perfect forms the Law can take. The perfection of the Law is the perfection of the pact that annuls it: yet another way of being perfectly faithful to Kant. This time, however, faithfulness to the modern image of the Law is faithfulness to its first aspect, the aspect of its foundation. The pact that finds itself at the centre of the Law is what bars the path of the Law towards foundation and renders the paradox of its grounding itself in its form fully untenable. A bit like the figures in Kafka, Bartleby the scrivener manifests what Kant could not; but unlike in Kafka, this manifestation takes place in the run-up. This is Bartleby's sadism, but a sadism rid of the obsession with smashing: rather than smashing the founding of the Law, it suffices to replace the founding of the Law with the truth of the Law. And contrary to what is the case in Kafka, this truth is not the truth of desire: it is the truth of the Law's tautological character. Rather than an inversion, Bartleby practises the substitution of the pact for the Law: he practises the *conversion* of the Law.

28 Bartleby III   Just as there is something of Lewis Carroll in Kafka, we might say, there is something of Buster Keaton or Harold Lloyd in Bartleby. When the facade of an entire house falls on Buster Keaton in *Steamboat Bill, Jr.*, the open attic window allows him to pass through unharmed (on Keaton: C1, 173–7). Likewise, when the Law that governs labour relations is threateningly brandished by his employer, all Bartleby has to do is brandish his formula for the threat to collapse immediately. Yet unlike Buster Keaton, Bartleby does not emerge from this attempt at substituting the pact for the Law unscathed. At the end of Melville's story, he lets himself die in prison, thereby showing, perhaps, the inextricable, complicitous relation that his attempted operation entertains with the Law such as it is applied. Perhaps, though, this final victory of the Law (as, incidentally, in Kafka) is but one more way of making it fail. Because it always triumphs, the Law cannot but expose itself ever more to the paradox that constitutes it and that presents an image of perfection which the Law itself is unable to believe in. Hence the lawyer's regrets, mixed with relief, when he learns of Bartleby's death: bad conscience has a way of wearing you down. The game of cat and mouse that characterises the comic manifested by Bartleby's formula, too, can thus be given a name. It is no longer irony, as in Sade, but something else, closer to a gag, something like slapstick. Bartleby is the silent and empty hub around which an ever more crazed Law is spinning, entirely by itself, like a hysteric. What Bartleby's formula enounces is this hysteria of the founding, a hysteria that sheds light on the Kantian bad conscience that ought one day to be explained.

29 *Agamben* In his short study of 'Bartleby', Giorgio Agamben takes a position that is rather close to that of Deleuze. For Agamben, Bartleby is the figure that best embodies the notion of 'decreation'. Once the scrivener is seen as a scribe in the evangelic sense, Bartleby's renunciation of writing becomes a renunciation of the Law as well: the irruption of Bartleby and his formula is there 'to fulfill the Torah by destroying it from top to bottom'.[8] And this destruction, Agamben explains, takes the form of 'an experiment *de contingentia absoluta*',[9] that is to say, of experimenting with reversing the principles of the past's irrevocability and of conditioned necessity that, according to Aristotle, govern all creation. Against these two principles, '"I would prefer not to' is the *restitutio in integrum* of possibility, which keeps possibility suspended between occurrence and nonoccurrence, between the capacity to be and the capacity not to be.'[10] Since the order of the Law is the order of the irrevocable and the necessary, the reversal of this order operated by Bartleby's formula is the affirmation of the pure possible. Bartleby's formula is not only an instrument for critiquing the law, it is also an instrument of liberation from the hold the Law has on us. Yet this liberation is strictly negative: it aims to operate the breaking of the chains by which Bartleby finds himself bound to necessity. For Agamben, there must be something like the *possibility of a possibility* not conditioned by the circumstances in which it arises: a pure event without coordinates. It is this naked possibility that Bartleby's formula embodies, a possibility whose positive formulation is impossible, on pain of being recaptured by what one seeks thereby to escape. This is Bartleby's Zen attitude: his not willing.

30 Zourabichvili   Gilles Deleuze himself associates humour with a certain notion of Zen: the comic of the event is the comic of the freedom of its coming. Neither foreseeable nor surprising, the event is that for which we ought to get ready: there is a Deleuzian involuntarism here, a way of refusing all intervention – that, at least, is the thesis François Zourabichvili defends in a famous article.[11] According to him, the figure of Bartleby is indeed, as Agamben claims, a negative figure, the figure of a foundering of the Law refusing all positive intervention against it. It is the Law itself that collapses, and it collapses on its own: Bartleby is neither the agent of this collapse nor even its spectator, circumstance, or occasion. Bartleby's formula is stochastic: it happens that he would prefer not to and it happens that the Law collapses. David Rabouin has criticised this involuntarism, citing the problematic character of the link between Zen and Bartlebyism. There is a virtuosity of Zen that allows for putting Zen on trial when this virtuosity puts itself in the service of something else (as in the case of the Japanese kamikaze, for example). Similarly, involuntarism is a mastery that can never just be considered in a purely negative way. Bartleby is responsible for what he does: a necessity comes back where necessity was thought to have been evacuated. But is this so evident? It would not be the case if Bartleby desired to make the law collapse itself,

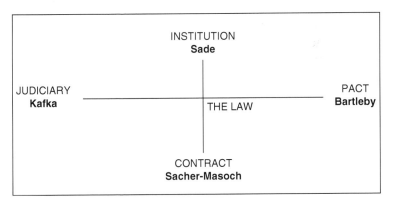

Figure 2 First diagram of the critique of the modern thinking of the Law

which is not the case. That is the stochastic character of his formula: it is content with expressing something (the nullity of the Law) that takes place separately from it and in which it takes no part. If Bartleby is anything, then he is the means the Law itself makes use of to turn itself into a laughing stock or a slapstick stage set. Where Rabouin is right, however, is that Bartleby is very voluntarist in the pronouncement of his formula: he sticks to his pact with all he has – that the Law does not make it is but the involuntary consequence of this voluntarism.

31 Exfoliation, invagination We must make a distinction. On the one hand, Sade and Sacher-Masoch operate, respectively, the perversion and the subversion of the Law by taking recourse to institutions and to contracts. On the other hand, Kafka and Bartleby operate, respectively, the inversion of the Law and its conversion by inscribing it in the assemblage of justice and in the pact at the core of the Law. There are thus *two great modes* of reversing the modern thinking of the Law of which Kant made himself the spokesman. There is first its reversal by exfoliation on a level that, in expressing the truth of its form, renders the paradoxical character of the Law unliveable. But there is also its reversal by *invagination*, that is to say, by widening this paradox at the very heart of the Law. Kafka and Bartleby are not only concerned with rendering the Law unliveable by affirming the unliveable character of the paradox that constitutes it. They are also concerned with pushing this paradox to the point where it loses all consistency and degenerates into ridicule. In *Coldness and Cruelty* (as well as, incidentally, in *Logic of Sense*), Deleuze thus presents only one half of the modes in which the critique of the modern thinking of the Law can operate. These modes are in fact much more numerous than the modes of the critique of the classical thinking of the Law. We must note, though, that the situation there is also much simpler: on the side of classical thinking, a comic immanent to the Law already contributes to problematisating its found-

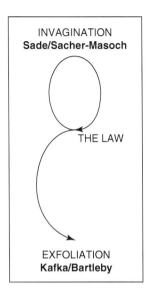

Figure 3 Diagram of the critique of the modern thinking of the Law

ing (Plato), while on the side of its critique, this comic finds itself expressed in a mode that subordinates the Law to its problematisation. Once the modern thinking of the Law finds itself in the paradoxical situation in which it claims to evacuate its comic proper in order to finally manage its serious foundation, the shattering of this foundation could not but take, in keeping with the thermodynamic laws of intellectual life, a more explosive form.

32 Critique I   We can now return to the critical character of the critique of the thinking of the Law. Dividing the history of thinking the Law into the thinking itself and its critique implies a certain conception of critique. What is critiquing the Law? Perhaps we have to make a distinction. First, it is possible to critique the Law in the *criticist*, that is to say Kantian, sense of the word. According to this first sense, critiquing the Law is the very operation of its instauration: the operation of subordinating it to a judgement that rises above it. This is the operation of Kant's philosophical subjection of the law, which Jean-Luc Nancy has analysed so well.[12] But this operation, as we now see, has failed. There is also a second sense of critique, which is that of *deconstruction* or destruction. This is the sense Jacques Derrida defends when he sees in justice the great deconstructor of law.[13] Once again Kantian, Derrida's concern is with operating a subjection borne by a philosophical demand: all laws worthy of the name conform to THE LAW. Yet unlike Kant's, the subjection Derrida wishes for is not a judgement: justice does all the work, we merely have to record it prudently. Finally, there is a third sense of critique, which is that of *denunciation*: according to this position, critiquing or criticising amounts to submitting the Law to its own weakness. Yet this is once again to trust the Law too much, namely, this time, its consequences, and to still be Kantian. As if there were something to denounce in the Law that it does not denounce itself: there is nothing to denounce in the Law since what remains of the Law once it is left to itself is precisely nothing at all. Neither criticism, nor deconstruction, nor denunciation, the critique Deleuze is referring to might be the critique of the process by which the Law manifests its vanity: a process of vanishing.

33 Critique II We must once again make a distinction. Gilles Deleuze in fact defines *critique* as an 'art of combinations [*conjugaisons*]' opposed both to the 'art of declension', which constitutes the *clinic*, and to the absence of art, as in criticism, deconstruction, or denunciation. These latter, in fact, still belong too much to the logic of the Law's own 'plane of organization': it prevents the birth of something like a 'plane of consistence' where the Law could become anything other than a principle of organisation (*D*, 89–91). Critique in the sense Deleuze practises it is precisely the attempt to elaborate such a plane of consistence that, meanwhile, does not owe critique anything. The Law, institutions, contracts, and justice in themselves deploy the possibility of a plane of consistence that description can record. Yet such a critique constitutes only half the path: it still does not lead anywhere; it still does not set out in search of anything. Let's say that it is the condition of a possible clinic: critiquing the Law, for Deleuze, amounts to establishing the necessity to exit the Law to be able to give it an interesting signification. This signification, though, takes a different form to the form of the Law itself: we must invent an outside of the Law for the Law not to be null. And this outside cannot be the outside of the ironist who only takes the Law's plane of organisation to a different level: as such, there is no plane of consistence of the Law since the plane of organisation is precisely the plane of the Law. There is a contamination of the Law and of the paradox that constitutes it in everything that belongs to the order of 'the development of forms and the formation of subjects'. That is why the critique of the thinking of the Law is above all a deployment of this paradoxical status at its greatest extension: a description of the Law always constitutes a 'plane of transcendence' that is its secret, as it were, albeit a secret of little value (*D*, 91–2).

34 The Law   There is thus a vanity of the Law. Yet what Law does this critique address? Because Deleuze is not concerned with denouncing it, the Law does not receive from him any other characterisation than as 'priest' (*D*, 89).[14] But we must understand this in the Nietzschean sense of the priest as someone who explains everything with something else, who annuls everything by subsuming it under something that would be superior. This Law can thus be, indifferently, juridical, psychoanalytic, anthropological, or even scientific. What is important is the plane of organisation it constitutes and which traverses a multiplicity of practices in order to correlate them with a lack. There must be Law because God, justice, truth are not on this earth: all we have as our horizon are finitude, melancholia, and death. Yet for Deleuze, all that, despicable as it may be, is of little importance: he is interested only in what it produces and how it works. In *A Thousand Plateaus* he thus puts forward the notion of the Law as a 'compars': as a plane of organisation, it aims at 'extracting constants, even if those constants are only relations between variables (equations)'. The Law is what organises the multiple, that is to say, not only what orders it but what prevents its proliferation: under the regime of the Law, there are no multiplicities of multiplicities, there is only *one* multiplicity in which everything comes together. That this multiplicity is such from the point of view of psychoanalysis, of anthropology, of religion, of science, or of law is, ultimately, contingent. It is always the same Law but expressed in different modes: this thing that 'still "savors of morality"' (*TP*, 369–70). The critique of the thinking of the Law whose history or diagram Deleuze traces, while it appears at the intersection of law and morality, in fact holds for all forms of Law since those forms are the same (*AO*, 212–17).

35 Daddy–Mommy Deleuze nonetheless makes a distinction between two aspects of the Law that, once again, allows for classifying the critiques addressed to it. He distinguishes between the Law in the mommy sense and the Law in the daddy sense. To the Law understood as *Daddy* corresponds the idea that there is a principle to which everything ought to be subordinate. The daddy-law is the Law that says, *Follow my example, I love you, or you'll be punished*. To the Law understood as *Mommy*, inversely, corresponds the idea that there is something that exists in order to be responsible in our place for what we do. The mommy-law, then, is the one that says, *Let me handle things, I love you, I know what is good for you*.[15] That all Law has a relationship with the symbolic universe of the family and the Oedipal triangulation that constitutes it must thus be understood from an immanent point of view. The symbolic LAW is a point of view onto the Law, a point of view that breaks down into a mommy-figure that, as in Sade and Sacher-Masoch, is to be overthrown (by knocking the Mother down or, on the contrary, replacing her with a better Mother), and into a daddy-figure that, as in Kafka and Melville, is to be overthrown as well (by inflating the Father to the point of absurdity or, on the contrary, decomposing him to the point of insignificance).[16] The critique of the thinking of the Law is also the critique of the possibility that a Law superior to the Law should redeem it: the juridical Law and the symbolic Law are on the same level; they say the same thing, they do the same thing, but in different places. It is thus possible to cover the domain of the one starting from the other and vice versa: it is possible, by decomposing the Father, to make the juridical thinking of the Law collapse all at once. Sometimes, that's even the best thing to do.

36 Young girls   Faced with the general ruin of the Law – a ruin that is its own, that of the assemblage in which it is inscribed, and that of the possibility of another Law – what remains? If the plane of organisation does not hold, where do we turn – if not to the plane of consistence? Why is there Law and why is the world not convulsing in laughter each time it is invoked? That is a bad question: *why*, that's still the Law speaking. We must ask *how*: how do we deal with the Law? We can laugh. But laughter implies a lot of things. Sade, Sacher-Masoch, Kafka and Bartleby, when they laugh, always have someone to turn to. According to Deleuze, that someone is, in each case, a *young girl*: Sacher-Masoch's oral mothers; Sade's incestuous girls; the sisters, maids, and whores in Kafka; the brothers and sisters in Melville.[17] There is the laughter of the young girls we also find in Proust that embodies the possibility of a flight outside of what is playing the all-too-ordered game of the Law and its critique. The young girls, in Deleuze, never critique: they help or they rescue. But this help and this rescue are not abstract or mystical, they are concrete and pragmatic. The young girls suggest metamorphoses that are so many ways of no longer letting oneself be captured by the Law's plane of organisation.[18] This, incidentally, might be the supreme form of its reversal: rather than try to continue to pervert the Law, to subvert it, to invert it, or to convert it, it might quite simply be better to be diverted by it. The comic proper to the Law would thus lose its bitterness and allow for turning towards a territory

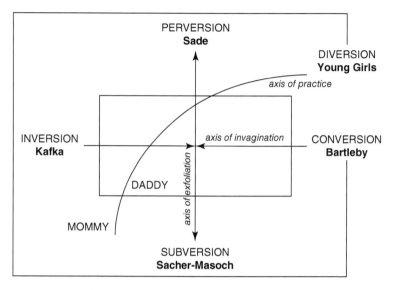

Figure 4 Second diagram of the critique of the modern thinking of the Law

where its importance would be, would always have been, null. Even at the centre of his harshest critique, Deleuze hints at this territory: it is the territory of law.

Notes

1. This and the following quotations, CC, 81–2.
2. See 'En guise de conclusion: La nuit la plus longue: Sade et Portalis au pied de l'échafaud' in Ost, Sade et la loi, 281–323.
3. See also LS, 243: 'Such is the most general mechanism of perversion, on the condition that perversion be distinguished as an art of the surface from subversion as a technique of depth.'
4. See also K, 10–11, 41–2 (and note 16), and elsewhere, as well as 'Re-presentation of Masoch', ECC, 53–5, here 54. But also see K, 66–7, on the difference between Kafka and Sacher-Masoch.
5. Compare Derrida, Before the Law.
6. See Cacciari, Icone della legge, 58–143.
7. See 'Bartleby; or, The Formula', ECC, 68–90.

8. Agamben, 'Bartleby', III.6:270.
9. Agamben, 'Bartleby', III.1:261.
10. Agamben, 'Bartleby', III.5:267.
11. See Zourabichvili, 'Deleuze et le possible'.
12. See Nancy, 'Lapsus iudicii'.
13. See Derrida, 'Force of Law', 14–15.
14. See also *SPP*, 106–7, on the 'mystification of laws'.
15. On 'mommy-territoriality and the daddy-law', see *AO*, 277.
16. See, respectively, *CC*, 90 and 47–56; *K*, 9–15; and *ECC*, 84–6.
17. See, respectively, *CC*, 94–5 and 59–60; *K*, 65–6; and *ECC*, 87–90.
18. See *AO*, 95–6. See Appendix 1 for a more detailed discussion of the rule of the young girls in Deleuze's development of a 'juridical pornology'.

II

Clinic

1 Thesis II The thesis that constitutes the second component of Deleuze's philosophy of law is enounced in the proposition, 'Jurisprudence is the philosophy of law, and deals with singularities, it advances by working out from singularities' (N, 153). Unlike the first, which defines a history, this second thesis is inscribed in a form of contemporaneity. Deleuze articulates it in a conversation with François Ewald and Raymond Bellour on the general theme of philosophy, in the course of a larger elaboration on the becoming of the contemporary world and the crisis of law that characterises it. Deleuze presents this crisis of law in several ways. There is, first, the distinction between disciplinary societies and control societies developed in the famous 'Postscript'. Then there is, second, the distinction between 'apparent acquittal' and 'unlimited postponement' he proposes in a synthetic article on Kant. And then, finally, there is the overview of contemporary law in *What is Philosophy?*, with an emphasis on the question of human rights.[1] In all three cases, the diagnosis is similar: there is a contemporary situation of the law, which is one of crisis and distinct from its past situation. It is this crisis that Deleuze articulates when he defines contemporary society as a control society marked by an unlimited postponement that is best expressed by the esteem of this society for human rights. In formulating his second thesis, Deleuze presents an exposé of this situation of crisis and at the same time a way of exiting it. Rather than further advance the critique he engages in with the first thesis, it is necessary to proceed to the clinic.

2 Discipline What exactly does the crisis from which law suffers consist in? In his conversation with Ewald and Bellour, but also in a different interview with Antonio Negri, Deleuze gives several examples of domains of law affected by this crisis: penal law in its relation to the prison, the development of law pertaining to biology, and so on (*N* 153 and 169–70). In all these domains, what is being questioned is an old world of functioning characterised by a certain image of the Law. This image of the Law was the one embodied by the modern thinking of the Law (Kant): the image of a Law that found its founding (the Good) and its justification (the Best) in its form. Thanks to this old image of the Law, law was able to contribute to the elaboration of what Deleuze, taking up an expression of Foucault's, calls 'discipline societies'. In discipline societies, life unfolds shaped by constant detention, by passing from one closed place to another: from family to school, from school to army, from army to work, and so on. Yet this passage from one regime of detention to another takes the form of sliding from one apparent acquittal to another: one is always guilty of something else, which justifies a new detention. This apparent acquittal, which is in reality an ever-renewed culpabilisation, characterises the thinking of the Law developed by Kant; Freud summarises it in the notion of 'bad conscience'. For a long time, we have lived in societies marked by this bad conscience, and law, because it was called on to accord with the image of the Law deployed by thinking, has contributed to it with its specific kind of violence, a violence of which Deleuze says, in *A Thousand Plateaus*, that it takes the form of a policing that resembles the 'State policing' characteristic of the state of law (*TP*, 448).

3 Control If there is a crisis of law, it is because this old definition of law as 'State policing' no longer holds. In entering the age of 'control societies', the modern image of the Law is being questioned, and with it the logic of apparent acquittal to which it gave rise. In contemporary society, in fact, detention no longer exists. Or, rather, it no longer exists in the discontinuous form of passing from one detention institution to another. In societies of control, detention is diffuse: the proclamation of guilt or the acquittal we continue to expect never arrive. We henceforth find ourselves in a state that is no longer that of apparent acquittal but that of 'unlimited postponement', that is to say, the state of a culpability that is all the more profound and enduring for our unawareness of its source and cause. In a way, Deleuze specifies, societies of control no longer embody the modern image of the Law but that of its critique. We no longer live under a Kantian power but under a Kafkaian power. This power must not be understood as an abstract and unjust machine but as a concrete machine of justice: in Kafka, you'll recall, we find *actualised* what in Kant is only expressed in the form of an unsayable paradox. From the point of view of the Law, 'control societies' in this sense must be considered hyper-Kantian. Hence the crisis of law, whose modern practice rests precisely on its remaining silent about this paradox. The bad conscience of modern law inexorably transforms into cynicism, a State cynicism of which Peter Sloterdijk has painted a farcical portrait.[2]

4 Crisis   In Deleuze's view, nothing embodies this passage from a logic of apparent acquittal to a logic of unlimited postponement better than the trust control societies place in human rights. Deleuze's severity concerning human rights is as impressive as Marx's in *On the Jewish Question*: there are no words harsh enough to castigate the stupidity of philosophers who make themselves their defenders.[3] Yet where Marx saw in human rights a bourgeois mystification dissimulated under appeals to the humanity of the human (Marx still belonged to discipline societies), Deleuze by contrast sees a capitalist mystification dissimulated under a critique of the bourgeois mystification. 'Human rights', Deleuze writes, 'say nothing about the immanent modes of existence of people provided with rights' (*WP*, 107). What is revolting about human rights is not that they seek to impose on everyone what only few benefit from (that would be paternalism); it is rather that what they seek to impose is in fact a curse. When benefiting from rights is the condition for entering societies in which control is exercised precisely through the Kafkaian craze typical of them, human rights evince the programme of an unlimited postponement. There is, Deleuze writes, a shame of being human, a shame that expresses itself not only in extreme situations (those described by Primo Levi) but above all in those that belong to the most ordinary every-dayness. Instead of marking a progress of law, human rights constitute the major example of its crisis: henceforth, law is nothing anymore, the Law has gained the upper hand, this formal Law whose last word is expressed by the Kantian morality from which it flows.

5 *Clinic* We must liberate *law* from *the Law*, that is to say, liberate law from philosophy: this is the clinical agenda Deleuze adopts. Despite the severity of his remarks about the contemporary world, he prefers not to elaborate on them: keeping one's distance from sad affects in order to give full space to joyous affects – here, as always, Spinoza's watchword applies. Deleuze prefers to be interested in the way in which, despite everything, something of law subsists underneath the Law – since, as a result of his critique, the Law is unable to stand on its own and keeps foundering, it must logically be the case that something of law persists even at the core of the contemporary ignominy. Where critique, in keeping with Nietzsche's wishes, is joyful destruction, clinic for its part must unfold as joyful construction. Zourabichvili has isolated the different traits of the clinical agenda that traverses Deleuze's thinking. The operations of this agenda, of the 'formation of a progressive and creative disorgani-zation', are taxonomy, cartography, immanent evaluation, and the 'sensitive and patient decipher[ing] of the regimes of signs that existence produces'.[4] Clinic is not the inverse of critique but its simultaneous flipside: the clinic is running

at the same time as the critique is operating. In other words, at the same time as the history of the thinking of the Law is being critiqued as comic through and through, it liberates a laughter that is foreign to it and produces something like its counter-history. Laughter, you'll recall, is the innocent and crystalline laughter of the young girls in Proust that the Law, be it daddy-Law or mommy-Law, will never manage to silence. Just as there is a history of the thinking of the Law, so there is a history of what is absolutely disjoint from it, and this is the history – or rather a genealogy – of the practice of law, a practice as foreign to the Law as it is to control.

6 *Axiomatics*   According to Deleuze, the history of the practice of law has three moments. The first moment is what we might call *pre-law*: this moment corresponds to the domination of a custom whose law, if it exists, is never anything but an exacting expression. The second is the *topical* moment of law: this moment corresponds to the development of a casuistic practice without concepts whose most accomplished expression is Roman law. The third is the *axiomatic* moment of law: the moment of systematising and abstracting the topical practice in larger sets, perfectly summed up by the enterprise of codification (*TP*, 451–2 and 569n44). According to Deleuze, the crisis of law erupts at the very core of this axiomatic moment of law. To the axiomatic moment of law corresponds, from the political point of view, the emergence of discipline societies whose existence is now questioned by their transformation into control societies. Yet we must understand that the crisis of law is not a crisis of its axiomatic character. On the contrary, it is the purest and most accomplished expression thereof. There is, Deleuze affirms, a misunderstanding about the idea of a code. When it comes to the enterprises of codification, we would do better not to speak of codes but of *decoding*. The overcoding of custom proper to pre-law and the encoding of cases proper to the topical practice of law are succeeded by an enterprise

of decoding concepts that pushes law to become an axiomatic system. The expression 'axiomatic' must be taken literally: the enterprise of codification aims indeed to construct an abstract logical system whose coherence is ensured solely by its conformity to the axiomatic form that is its own, which is that of the contemporary world (*TP*, 453, on the 'general axiomatic of decoded flows').

7 *Code* In mathematical logic, there are rules that apply to the way in which axioms are formed and manipulated: codes submit to these rules. It is in this manner that a 'code' like the *Code civil* can be understood to embody the axiomatic logic of modern law in a privileged way. Three traits in particular express this point: '(1) the predominance of the enunciative form over the imperative and over affective formulas (damnation, exhortation, admonishment, etc.); (2) the code's pretension that it forms a complete and saturated rational system; (3) but at the same time the relative independence of the propositions, which permit axioms to be added' (*TP*, 569n50). From this point of view, the enterprise of codification can be described as the triumph of decoding over encoding, the triumph of concepts over cases, and the triumph of abstraction over practice. What characterises the axiomatic practice of law is its simultaneously formal and transcendent character: not only does the form of law determine the content of law but this form is no longer juridical except by decree, a decree we might call philosophical. In Kant, the Law takes an axiomatic form since what it expresses is the same thing as the way in which it expresses it – namely that, formally, it is indeed a Law. That is why, once the crisis of contemporary law presents itself as the Kafkaian actualisation of the modern thinking of the Law, the axiomatic practice that corresponds to it, for its part, is confirmed by this crisis as well. The crisis of law, in this sense, would be but a growth crisis of this axiomatic practice and thus the sign that new progress towards a more advanced axiomatics is to be expected. But, in another sense, it is just as possible

to say that there is a crisis of law because its axiomatisation does not succeed in completing itself.

8 Problems   The axiomatisation of law runs into four *problems* that testify to the incongruence of the thinking of the Law and the practice of law. These problems are *legalism, naturalism, consensualism,* and *institutionalism.* These four problems feature a similar structure: one of the constitutive elements of the practical implementation of the thinking of the Law turns out, in each case, to be a constitutive element of its concrete betrayal. Not only does the thinking of the Law not manage to bring itself about in a logical and coherent whole; its implementation turns out to be just as unfaithful to its programme. And these are very much concrete problems; they are not new dimensions of the critique of the thinking of the Law. There is in Deleuze something like a philosophy of the problem, which comes straight from Bergson. As Deleuze, evoking Bergson, reminds us, a problem is not a difficulty: the issue is not to show that the practical implementation of the modern thinking of the Law encounters obstacles that it would suffice to overcome for the implementation to become possible. A problem is something that is created, all at once and in its entirety: the concern in inventing a problem is with widening a difference rather than with restoring a unity (*B,* 15–17). In fact, whether it be legalism, naturalism, consensualism, or institutionalism, the problems properly belonging to the axiomatic practice of law that Deleuze enjoyed creating establish a difference with the Law within the Law itself. And, by way of consequence, they establish the Law itself as the perfect example of a false problem, that is, one that from the practical point of view does not result in the creation of any difference. Once again, from the point of view of law, the existence or inexistence of the Law is of no consequence at all.

9 Legalism   There is a *first* problem: the legalism at the core of the axiomatic practice of law. Deleuze credits Foucault with having invented this problem, which he articulates as follows: according to the modern thinking of the Law, the Law takes its consistence from opposing itself to the illegality it is fighting against. Yet what we observe in examining the societies where the modern thinking of the Law serves as programme is that this distinction explains none of the aspects of the juridical practice it supposedly governs. The distinction *Law – illegality* is to be replaced with the finer distinction of *Law – illegalisms*, in which the opposition is no longer between a positive and a negative but between several forms of negativities. 'Law is always a structure of illegalisms, which are differentiated by being formalized' (*F* 29). In the axiomatic practice of law, two things are at issue: on the one hand, creating illegalisms (there is no illegalism without Law) and, on the other, differentiating them (all illegalisms are not equal). This differentiating creation can take place according to three modalities: permission, tolerance, and prohibition, which do not apply in the same way or to the same people. In the axiomatic practice of law that corresponds to the emergence of discipline societies, what is allowed some is not allowed others and vice versa. Deleuze takes the example of the invention of commercial law: 'We need only look at the law of commercial societies to see that laws are not contrasted worldwide with illegality, but that some are actually used to find loopholes in others' (*F*, 29). In other words, in differentiating, illegalisms end up themselves finding loopholes in the Law with the blessing of the Law. By creating a close-meshed web of illegalisms, the Law produces much more than exceptions: defining an illegalism becomes a means of legalising.

10 Intervention From the point of view of the axiomatic practice of law, legalism is a false problem: an infraction of the Law never explains anything, neither about the infraction itself nor about the Law it breaks. Legalism is one of the aspects of an axiomatics, understood as a model of thinking that provides law with a homogeneity that it did not even claim. Illegalism, in turn, allows for explaining why, in practice, law passes through a multiplicity of strategies to penetrate the relationships between Law and illegalisms that, in its view, are the only ones to be of interest. The practice of law is not one of applying a model but one of drawing up a map or blueprint; and it is not one of implementing the Law but of describing strategies (*F*, 30). Nietzsche, too, discusses this point highlighted by Foucault. It is stupid, Nietzsche explains, to consider the Law as the application of a force, be it that of an individual or that of the State: it must still be said what type of force is at issue. There are also active forces that intervene in the definition of illegalisms and that sketch trajectories freed from the weight of the Law onto the map of these illegalisms (*NP*, 133–4). Justifying the Law by its opposition to illegality, in consequence, amounts to not justifying it at all: if it is content with chasing after illegality, the Law is unjustifiable. The only justification it could know would be to permit interventions at the centre of a map that goes beyond it on all sides. There is a terrorist use of the Law, which is the use the axiomatic practice of law makes of it. Following this terrorist use, the issue is no longer about producing an abstract justification of the Law but of testing the pertinence of a concrete *intervention* within the tangle of illegalisms, for example: displacing a prohibition, making a permission more difficult, or inverting the beneficiaries of prohibitions and permissions.

11 Diagram Following Foucault, Deleuze develops the example of penal law at length (*F*, 31). In *Discipline and Punish*, Foucault describes the historical emergence of a new carceral universe he calls 'the great lockup', which also corresponds to the emergence more broadly of discipline societies.[5] The development of penal law at the beginning of the age of discipline societies responded to a very precise necessity: to bring about, by putting the logic of punishment into axioms, something like social peace (*F*, 33). In a way, this social peace – based on the defence of society against the evils it secretes, the transformation of the condemned into a normal human being, the modulation of punishment as a function of the gravity of the act, and the individuation of the act as a function of the circumstances that surround it – constituted the content of the Law that programmed it. Yet what resulted, according to Foucault, was something else: not social peace but a veritable production of prisons and prisoners that keep feeding demand for social peace. This, however, does not warrant the conclusion that penal law is a failure: what counts, on the contrary, is that it enounces and renders visible a multiplicity of differences in matters of crime and criminals that would have remained invisible without it. The *programme* of the Law, which still allows for imputing who decides and who is responsible, is replaced by a *diagram* of law, which keeps refining impersonal differences. There is no diagram of penal Law since there must be someone to enounce it; but there is a diagram of penal law once the ramifications of the operations it permits unfurl outside all imputation. The axiomatic practice of law is no more an arbitrary practice than it is a practice of force: it is a practice of the 'particular [*quelconque*]' (F, 34).

12 *Naturalism I* The *second* problem proper to the axiomatic practice of law is that of naturalism, which Deleuze credits Spinoza with inventing, albeit based on its earlier invention by Lucretius. Lucretius poses the problem of naturalism in the topical practice of law, and Spinoza reformulates it from the point of view of its axiomatic practice. In a lecture course from 1980 that remained unpublished, Deleuze defines two different moments of naturalism: a classical moment, embodied by Cicero, and a modern moment, embodied by Hobbes (S; *EPS*, 258–60). Naturalism, Deleuze explains, is a relationship established between the practice of law and the thinking of the Law, a constituting relationship anchoring one in the other. The problem of naturalism is no longer that of justifying the practice of law but that of its foundation or its founding: in what way can a practice of law be said to

be founded in the Law? Classical natural law, through the voice of Cicero, answers this question in four propositions: (a) Naturalism is an *essentialism*: the anchoring of law in the Law is equivalent to its anchoring in the very essence of things, which in the case of the human being is rationality. (b) Naturalism is a *socialism*: the anchoring of law in the nature of the human being implies that the society that develops law is the only one to be in conformity with natural law (the state of nature is not pre-social). (c) Naturalism is a *functionalism*: the moment that the task is to actualise the rational essence of the human in a good society, law becomes a composite of duties. (d) Naturalism is an *elitism*: the wise man makes a political claim, since he is the only one to have access to the knowledge of the nature of the human and of the society consubstantial with it.

13 Naturalism II   What characterises the axiomatic practice of law is that this relation that binds law to the Law has transformed. Hobbes reverses the four constitutive propositions of classical natural law. For Cicero's formulations, Hobbes substitutes new ones that aim to separate law from all essence. (a) Hobbes argues that contrary to what Cicero claimed, the nature of things is not an essence but a *power*. 'All you can do is permitted, that is natural law', Deleuze says (*S*). This implies, (b) that the state of nature is not a social state but what precedes the social state, given that the social state is a state of limitations and prohibitions. Society, too, is not a problem of essence but a problem of *becoming*. In consequence, (c) the duties owed to society are replaced by *rights* that this same society limits. Law is no longer indexed by duty: it becomes the operator of a social becoming that places duties second. Thereby, (d) the wise man is deprived of the exclusive competency he could claim in political matters. On the contrary, in modern natural law, the wise man and the madman are equally entitled to intervene in them. The difference that exists between the wise man and the madman is no longer a question of nature (since in the state of nature, everyone is equal) but a question of society: it is society that decrees that some are competent while others are not. Yet the establishment of society, which is a question of becoming, rests on *consent* and not on expertise: the great idea of natural modern law is, as Deleuze puts it: 'Nobody is competent for me' (*S*). Even if Hobbes is concerned with anchoring the practice of law in the Law, this anchoring no longer takes place from the point of view of a decreed essence but from that of an active power.

14 Subvention   In its axiomatic practice, law has freed itself from essence, from wisdom, from conformity with the social state of things, and from the primacy of duties. This once more constitutes a problem from the point of view of the thinking of the Law. For Hobbes, this Law, too, is a naturalism – except that he interprets such naturalism in a completely different way. For Kant, the question natural law raises concerns the possibility of providing law with a foundation. Hobbes says exactly the same thing except that he does not provide a foundation: he provides a *subvention*. The issue in modern natural law is to establish modes of transforming law that not only go from a state of nature to a state of society but also from one state of society to another state of society. Naturalism is a plan of transformation: its Laws are no longer distinct from law but identical with it. In this sense, as Spinoza says, Laws become something like the norms of power: they provide support and direction, not in order to actualise this power (power is always real) but to extend it (*EPS*, 256). Gabriel Tarde articulated this extension in juridical terms, remarking, in *Les Transformations du droit* (*The Transformations of Law*), that law keeps enlarging itself both from the material and the personal point of view.[6] The axiomatic practice of law is the practice of the subvention of its enlargement to ever more domains and ever more people. Natural law opposes the thinking of the Law that always aims at bringing law back to a (moreover impossible) foundation with the definition of a world of subvention of the practice of law, a subvention that allows law to go ever further in its transformations. This mode of subvention is the mode of determining the natural Laws of the transformation of the powers that animate it.

15 Tarde   Of all other conceptions of law ever attempted, *Les Transformations du droit* may well present the one closest to that of Deleuze. In that book, Tarde sketches a philosophy of obligation and aims to apply to law the Laws of imitation that, according to him, make up the tissue of social life. These Laws of imitation constitute something like natural Laws if we accept that there is no natural law except as a generalisation of concrete operations. In Tarde's view, natural law in a way is nothing but a question of perspective. Where the concern is to turn natural law into the founding of positive law, this perspective is blurred. For Tarde, we must go back to the origin of natural law and the distinction within it between natural law in the strict sense and the *ius gentium*. The first, he explains, is a generalisation of the relationships within a group, whereas the second is a generalisation of groups' relationships with the members of other groups.[7] The interest of this distinction, according to Tarde, is of course that it calls for different technical consequences: a society is not extended the same way when this extension concerns the members of one and the same group as when it concerns members of different groups. Natural law and the *ius gentium* are the technical expressions of different ways of applying to law the Laws of imitation according to which the issue, in the domain of natural law, is always the power of an obligatory bond and its evolution. Natural law, in its two forms, claims from law a permanent evolution towards an increase of its field. But, in this sense, natural law is not a programme: the 'social teleology' that animates it is, first of all, a set of operations, a technical machine, whose goal is immanent to their functioning.

16 Composition   Yet there is in this naturalism of powers something more than what figures in Hobbes. Modern natural law, in fact, is too legal to accept the link between power and natural Laws. In his preface to Antonio Negri's *The Savage Anomaly*, Deleuze puts Hobbes back in a lineage that also includes Rousseau and Hegel. This lineage, which inherits from Hobbes, recognises itself in four theses that supplement those of its naturalism: '1) that forces have an individual or private origin; 2) that they must be socialised to bring about adequate relationships corresponding to them; 3) that there is thus mediation of a Power ("Potestas"); and 4) that the horizon is inseparable from crisis, war or antagonism that Power proposes to solve, though an "antagonist solution"' (*TRM*, 190). It is this power that Spinoza abandons: as Negri shows, Spinoza abandons *potestas* in favour of *potentia*, and thus mediation in favour of composition. The societies that natural Laws subvent are not regulated by the exercise of a power that would moreover play the role of a third. The decision about which directions the transformations of a society and of its law will take belongs to no one but those whom it concerns. But those whom it concerns, in order to make a society, must develop an entire process of *composition* that implies a multitude of relationships between power and power: individual as well as collective powers. Spinoza's naturalism, unlike Hobbes's, is not an individualism but a personalism: even the State has a power, implements it, and tends to extend itself by way of new concrete compositions, as Machiavelli shows.

17 Consensualism There is a *third* problem proper to the axiomatic practice of law: the problem of consensualism. The axiomatic practice of law is the practice of implementing the clauses of a contract that precedes it and whose form is the very form of the Law. With consensualism, law develops as a practice of the link, of the *nexum*, subjecting the person who binds herself to the obligations she contracts. Yet since consensualism is as old as the Law, which it thereby provides with an autogenous exterior guarantee, an outside that protects it from its own paradoxical character, it, too, has a history that is structured identically to that of the Law. Deleuze thus distinguishes between *three ages* of the contract. There is, first of all, 'the objective, imperial collective bond' that corresponds to the pre-law age and its overcoding of custom: the contract is concluded between a subject and a sovereign and aims to establish the Law of the sovereign as law that binds both parties. Second, there are 'all of the forms of subjective personal bonds' that correspond to the age of the topical practice of law: the contract establishes an equivalence of rights between the parties on the basis of a Law that escapes them both. Finally, there is 'the Subject that binds itself' that corresponds to the age of the axiomatic practice of law: individuals bind themselves to a Law which, however, no one asks them to obey or to follow (*TP*, 460). The history of consensualism is the history of the refinement of processes of subjectivation, that is to say, of subjective subjection to the Law, a subjection that is no more voluntary than it is coerced. Consensualism is the mode of existence of the Law once the Law is brought to the level of practices of law that implicate individuals. Legalism concerns *acts*, naturalism *society*: consensualism concerns *individuals*.

18 Convention The problem that the idea of a *nexum* introduces to the axiomatic practice of law is that of forgetting how these bonds work. From the point of view of the Law, consensualism is supposed to bind the individuals to their sovereign, to their neighbour, to themselves, and thus to the Law. But from the point of view of the practice of law, things are completely different: what interests the practice of law is not the fact that contracts bind but the way in which they bind. The *nexum* is thus first of all an institution that belongs to archaic Roman law, that defines itself as contract without *mancipatio*. In the *nexum*, the obligation arises from the word of the lender or giver, with no other specific trait than the magical-religious character of the institution itself (*TP*, 565n10). In consequence, other types of contracts, implying supplementary forms, oppose themselves to this *nexum*.

The practice of law keeps inventing new ways of fabricating bonds susceptible to producing new effects rather than always bringing back all bonds to the *nexum* to which the Law keeps appealing. As the relationship with the Law is refined, a way of agreeing [*convenir*] to bonds, too, is refined that has no relationship with the Law: bonds cobbled together in particular circumstances that have less to do with the contract and its obligations than with conventions and their artificial character. In practice, law keeps taking recourse to new forms of *conventions* that always aim to undo the bonds that exist between sovereign, individual and subject, and to reconfigure them differently. Rather than bonds, we have to speak of relationships here, a bit like Montesquieu: convention is the putting into relationship of heterogeneous elements rather than the ordering of elements postulated as homogeneous. In this sense, conventions, unlike contracts, never guarantee anything: conventions are no more negative than they are natural; they are positive and cultural (*ES*, 41–2).

19 Property Deleuze takes the example of property to express the difference between the consensualism of the thinking of the Law (contract) and that of the axiomatic practice of law (convention). Hume is the one who points out that property has nothing to do with a contract but everything, on the contrary, to do with a convention:

> The convention of property is the artifice by means of which the actions of each one are related to those of the others. It is the establishment of a scheme and the institution of a symbolic aggregate or of the whole. (*ES*, 42)

Property is not a contract consecrating the pre-existing rights and obligations that separate debtor from creditor, someone who cedes something from someone who receives something, or even a strong party from a weak one. It is a convention that, by means of defining new rights, brings these same individuals together in a totality composed of heterogeneous elements, a totality that would not exist without such a convention and the rights that serve as relationships there. Yet, according to Hume, property does not exist without the establishment of a totality of relationships: that is what property does from the practical point of view. In this sense, property is not conservative or limitative; it is creative and expansive. Just as natural Laws supported the possibility of a practice of law that drew the consequences of its own transformations, and just as the strategies of law consisted in intervening in an ever more complex and intricate map of illegalisms, so convention consists in permitting individuals to contribute to the composition of totalities that corresponds to what, among individuals, can be described as 'sympathy'. Convention is the translation, into the terms of the practice of law, of the morals of sympathy by which individuals construct their affective universes. For convention, '[t]he problem is how to *extend* sympathy' (*ES*, 40, Deleuze's emphasis).

20 Institutionalism There is, finally, a *fourth* problem of the axiomatic practice of law. It is that of the relationships between law and institutions. From the point of view of the thinking of the Law, these relationships must be thought as relationships of dependence: dependence vis-à-vis the State, society, the people, the economy, and so on. Institutions, from the point of view of the thinking of the Law, are the practical source of law and thus also the principle of the limitation of law: institutions are the organising frame of law. But these institutions change as a function of the age: it is only in the axiomatic practice of law that institutions are expected to serve as organising frames (*AO*, 179–271). Hume criticised this properly modern relationship that law entertains with institutions, and in *Empiricism and Subjectivity* Deleuze describes it as a chain of dependence. In organising law, institutions place themselves above it; yet since this organisation results from a demand of the Law, the Law supplants the institutions. Institutions are the expression of a rule of organisation that they do not master. In this sense, institutions are the *interfaces* of the concrete connection between the Law and law, and the *operators* of the concrete subjection of law to the Law. Nature was still a concept: the subjection of law to the Law at issue still interested only the Law. Institutions, by contrast, allow for ensuring this subjection even at the very core of the circumstances in which law seeks to escape the Law. Institutions are the police of law. In this sense, there is no institution that is not organising: it is possible to speak of institutions only when something like a police force is implemented.

21 Invention   But nothing could be more wrong. What Hume shows is that governmental institutions are not institutions: they are, in fact, nothing but bodies of police officers. We must differentiate between institutions and police officers. Institutions, Hume says, are strangers to the Law: they are general rules – the family, marriage, or, at bottom, property itself. But what is a general rule? It is 'a model of actions, a veritable enterprise, an invented system of positive means or a positive invention of indirect means' (*ES*, 45–6). Institutions are recognised by their possession of the *three traits* of every general rule: they are invented; they are means; and they are positive. That they are invented means that institutions derive from a practical activity, and certainly not from the Law. That they are means means that they have a goal to actualise. This goal comes from nowhere outside of them, and certainly not from the Law: it is an immanent goal. That they are positive means that this goal is not to limit or to organise but to contribute to what is already positive in society itself: the fact that it wants to extend itself. That is why an institution is a rule: not only is it extensive, it can also be corrective. There are corrective rules whose goal is to take care of the interstices of the extensions, the space of accidents and exceptions. Yet even corrective rules, even corrective institutions, are the juridical expression of the imagination or of *invention*. For Hume, in fact, the greatest inventors are not the great scientists but the great legislators: those who keep inventing new institutions as well as new developments for the existing institutions (*ES*, 40–1).

22 Legislation   The art of legislation is among the institutions that provoke the most misunderstandings. From the point of view of the thinking of the Law, legislation is an art of the State; its objective is the definition of rules that in turn aim to regulate the situations that fall within its field of application. From the point of view of government technique, legislation is often perceived as an instrument of a generalised pastoral: there are the good shepherds, the people of sheep, and the enclosures where the ones detain the others for their own good. Such a pastoral very much resembles the classical form of natural law: the naturalism of discipline societies is a late instance. Sometimes there are jurists to nuance and distinguish between different species of Laws: prohibitive, permissive, inciting, and so on – but that does not change anything: the aim of proclaiming Laws is always to be competent for others. When Hume makes the art of legislation an art superior to that of history's great scientists and grants legislators the honour of being greater inventors than scientists, he does not yield anything either to legalism, or to naturalism, or to consensualism. In Hume's view, the art of legislation is the art of inventing new relationships not only between individuals but between their actions, between the societies they compose and even between the institutions themselves. In this sense, the art of legislation is a paradoxical art: it requires at the same time the absence of a desire for reform and the presence of a desire for revolution. Reformism is a kind of debility, an incapacity to recognise the beauty of a state of things (Kant was reformist), whereas revolution is a sign of health: things are so beautiful that it is possible to go further. We must thus say: to be a great legislator is to be a revolutionary whose revolution consists in wanting to leave everything as it is – to leave everything untouched.

23 Practice   The axiomatic practice of law is thus fourfold. (a) It is first a practice of intervention (strategies) concerning acts (illegalisms). (b) It is then a practice of subvention (natural Laws) concerning societies. (c) It is also a practice of convention (artifices) concerning individuals. (d) It is finally a practice of invention (rules) concerning institutions. Under these four aspects, the axiomatic practice of law betrays the modern thinking of the Law to which, otherwise, it conforms. (a) It betrays first of all the idea of justification implied in the definition of the Law. (b) It then betrays the idea of foundation implied in the definition of natural law. (c) It also betrays the idea of guarantee implied in the definition of the contract. (d) It finally betrays the idea of limitation implied in the definition of government. There is thus a paradox that properly belongs to the axiomatic practice of law: on the one hand, it implements the programme that the modern thinking of the Law implies, but on the other, this implementation keeps getting further and further away from the terms of this programme. And yet the axiomatic practice of law claims to be faithful to the modern thinking of the Law: (a) there is Law in the interventions on the map of illegalisms; (b) there is Law in the subventions of societies actualised by the natural Laws; (c) there is Law in the conventions by which individuals bind themselves; and (d) there is Law in the inventions by which institutions extend the relationships that unite acts, societies, individuals and things. It therefore does not suffice to say that between the axiomatic practice of law and the modern thinking of the Law there is only the difference that always exists between a theory and a practice. At bottom, both constitute the same practice but seen from two different points of view: the thinking of the Law is its sad and sterile component

PROBLEM	PRACTICE	OBJECT	THINKING
Legalism	Intervention	Acts	Justification
Naturalism	Subvention	Societies	Founding
Consensualism	Convention	Individuals	Guarantee
Institutionalism	Invention	Institutions	Limitation

Figure 5 Overview of the axiomatic practice of law

whereas the axiomatic practice of law is its joyous and fertile component.

24 Logos   The axiomatic practice of law also changes the thinking of the Law. There are, in fact, two forms of Law: a Logos form and a Nomos form. The Logos form corresponds to the one embodied by the modern thinking of the Law where its object is what Deleuze calls the 'compars': 'The search for laws consists in extracting constants, even if those constants are only relations between variables (equations)' (*TP*, 369). The objective of the Logos, the legalist form of the Law, is not only the definition of a principle from which all axioms of the practice of law would then be deduced. It is also to reduce this practice to that which, within it, does not change. The strategy of the compars is a strategy of ignorance that passes itself off as a strategy of knowledge, since what it gives to know is precisely that on the basis of which all knowledge is made possible: the Law. Deleuze writes:

> There is one aspect, however concealed it may be, of the logos, by means of which the Intelligence always *comes before*, by which the whole is already present, the law already known before what it applies to: this is the dialectical trick by which we discover only what we have already given ourselves, by which we derive from things only what we have already put there. (*PS*, 105–6, Deleuze's emphasis)

Yet the strategy of the compars is also a strategy of sedentarisation: once what is changing is neglected in favour of what is not changing, the practice of law, compared with the thinking of the Law, cannot be satisfying insofar as it itself remains immobile. In the Logos form of the Law, the concern is with making law one of the 'pillars' of a society whose entire space is structured by immobile, parallel, and equivalent monoliths. And from a certain point of view it might be possible to say that the axiomatic practice of law pertains to the Logos and the compars: law always comes before the transgression, the solutions before the problems, the decision before the hesitation. But in that case, it is an axiomatic practice of *the Law*.

25 *Nomos*   Deleuze develops this line of reasoning in talking about Proust: the Kafkaian practice of the modern thinking of the Law does not constitute the entirety of this practice. There is something else: 'The depressive consciousness of the law as it appears in Kafka is countered in this sense by the schizoid consciousness of the law according to Proust' (*PS*, 132). Where the compars operates centripetally, there is also another operation at work that for its part is centrifugal: this is the 'dispars' to which corresponds a second form of the Law, no longer Logos but Nomos. Unlike the Logos, the Nomos is an adventure: the societies it governs are at the same time composed sets and the continual fragmentation, the dispersion, of this composition.

> [The L]aw in general, in a world devoid of the logos, controls the parts without a whole . . . And far from uniting or gathering them together in the same world, the law measures their discrepancy, their remoteness, their distance, and their positioning, establishing only aberrant communications between the noncommunicating vessels, transversal unities between the boxes that resists any totalization, inserting by force into one world the fragment of another world, propelling the diverse worlds and viewpoints into the infinite void of distances. This is why, on its simplest level, the law as social or natural law appears in terms of the telescope, not the microscope. (*PS*, 142–3)

Perhaps it is this dispars, pertaining to a 'schizoid consciousness' (*PS*, 132) of the Law, that haunts the axiomatic practice of law and makes it venture in the direction of intervention, subvention, convention, and invention rather than in the direction of justification, foundation, guarantee, and limitation. The axiomatic practice of law adopts the Nomos form of the Law by which it betrays the Logos form – without betraying the Law as such.

26 Schmitt   From this point of view, there is nothing more opposed to Deleuze's thinking than that of Carl Schmitt. In *The Nomos of the Earth*, Schmitt tries to reconstruct something like a lost normativity.[8] If it is no longer possible to graft law onto a moral or political idea, then it must be grafted onto the earth: it is the earth itself that becomes the source of all law. For Schmitt, the Nomos thus merges with the Logos – it respects and brings together more than it betrays and disperses. Yet for all that, Schmitt is acutely aware of the impossibility of sustaining such a Nomos without seeing it collapse eventually. Just like the Law whose telluric expression it sees itself as, the Nomos which he expects to *legitimate* law is an oxymoron. Schmitt's profound desire is to operate a return to the oldest and deepest sources of law to establish its axiomatisation more securely. In doing so, he ignores both the difference between Logos and Nomos and the difference between image of the Law and practice of law. In his view, the task is to render to law a compactness without seams, where law and Law, Logos and Nomos would keep on short-circuiting. It would have been permissible for him, however, to make use of the Nomos of the earth *against* the Logos of the Law. The earth, insofar as it is opposed to heaven and sketches the possibility of always new territories, is the exact opposite of the philosophers' heaven. It would have been possible to invent an axiomatic practice of law of the earth that would not have to pay tribute to the modern thinking of the Law. Yet Schmitt does not want to follow that path, anxious as he is to leave no opening for what to his mind is the most unbearable charge. This charge is precisely the one Deleuze decides to make the greatest quality of the axiomatic practice of law – namely, the accusation of betrayal.

27 Law   There are several ways of betraying the Law that correspond to the different modes of the axiomatic practice of law. Not all practices of law axiomatise in the same way: English law, German law and French law differ in that they privilege one aspect or another of this axiomatisation. In

What is Philosophy? Deleuze sketches a typology of modes of axiomatisation characterising the different practices of law in contemporary societies. 'English law is a law of custom and convention, as the French is of contract (deductive system) and the German of institution (organic totality)' (*WP*, 106). This typology must be understood as a way of operating solutions of continuity: a law [*un droit*] can one day be more French, more English another, and more German yet another day. (a) French law, the worst of all, trusts the Law too much in at least one of its points, which is the contract: it is too modern, not English enough. (b) German law, which is better, trusts less in the Law than in institutions: by axiomatising itself around institutions, it betrays the modern thinking of the Law on at least one point – it initiates its dispersion, even if it ends up in new totalities. (c) English law is the best: it is pragmatic from beginning to end, law that betrays the Law on at least one point, provided this point is more intense than the one that German law betrays. In English law, because it is one of customs and conventions, no totality ever results from exercising its dispositions. English law is almost pure Nomos, almost pure *dispars* – where German law is a mixture of Nomos and Logos and where French law is almost pure Logos, almost pure *compars*: law of the Code, thus law of decoded axioms. These are the three possible aspects of the axiomatic practice of law.

28 Topic Just as there is an axiomatic practice of law that corresponds to the modern thinking of the Law, there is thus a topical practice of law that corresponds to the classical thinking of the Law. This second kind of practice of law, which Deleuze distinguishes from the first in *A Thousand Plateaus*, is characterised by *three traits*: (a) its *modus operandi* (by conjunctions or associations); (b) its *modus pensierandi* (by *topos* or case); and (c) its *modus essendi* (by jurisprudence or casuistics). Yet the topical practice of law, Deleuze explains, is above all the practice of a certain age, of the end of the archaic imperial age and the beginning of the age of evolved empires, which spell themselves out in cities or feodalities and whose most important technical expression is Roman law. This epoch, too, is characterised by *three traits*. (a) First of all, the public sphere transforms: it 'no longer characterizes the objective nature of property but is instead the shared means for a now private appropriation'. (b) Next, the *nexum* transforms: '*The bond becomes personal*; personal relations of dependence, both between owners (contracts) and between owned and owners (conventions), parallel or replace community relations or relations based on one's public function.' (c) Finally, law transforms: it becomes 'subjective, conjunctive, "topical" law: this is because the State apparatus is faced with a new task, which consists less in overcoding already coded flows than *in organizing conjunctions of decoded flows as such*' (*TP*, 451, Deleuze and Guattari's emphases). The three characteristic traits of the topical practice of law correspond to this third transformation. The two other traits, subjectivation and appropriation, are relative, the one to the political regime, the other to the economic regime of the moment that opens with it. The axiomatic practice of law, for its part, relates to a politics of the particular and an economy of capital.

29 *Association*   The topical practice of law functions by conjunctions or *associations* rather than, as the axiomatic practice of law does, by conjugation. But what does functioning by conjunctions or associations mean? Once again, it is in talking about Hume that Deleuze makes a valuable observation. He writes: 'We expect that an arbitrator or a judge *would apply* the association of ideas and decree to which person or entity a thing is related inside the mind of an observer in general' (*ES*, 61, Deleuze's emphasis). In Deleuze's view, association is the method of law. Like all method, however, it is to be taken with caution: it is still too theoretical, not practical enough.[9] Following this method, law aims to establish relations, relationships, to compose associations between beings and between things. The difference

between association and conjugation lies in the type of bonds law seeks to establish: be it in a contract or in a convention, the axiomatic practice of law seeks to establish relationships concerned with something else. In contractual as well conventional relationships, politics and economics remain too close as preoccupations: law still depends too much on the one as on the other. In association, on the contrary, neither politics nor economics serve as standards for determining the value of a relationship. A juridical relationship is thus assessed on its capacity to link up with existing juridical relationships and to allow for producing new juridical relationships. The topical practice of law is a practice of operational chains: it is made up of nothing but successive associations and without any other determination than their technical robustness. It is a practice of *imputation*, as Bruno Latour has rightly noted, a practice whose techniques prove to be quite indifferent not only to the Law but to politics and economics themselves.[10]

30 Case I   The associations established by the topical practice of law are not general associations as was the case with the different forms of social contract. The topical practice of law is a practice of the *case*: it knows only concrete singularities. What is a case? A case is an accident. But what is an accident? It is, first of all, that which happens only once and without any other necessity than that of chance. It is, furthermore, that which despite happening only once changes everything: an accident is an upheaval. It is, finally, that which, because it upsets everything at once, requires being considered as such and being taken care of as such. It might be possible to define a case as what elsewhere Deleuze calls an event. But not all cases create an event: they are content with summoning the possibility of an event of which they are but the virtual endorsement. The topical practice of law cares very little about events, which it leaves to philosophers, activists, and historians: in law, there are no events, there are only cases. That is the reason why in the practice of law, each case, even cases that are banal and determined to remain banal, is as important as any other case. Since what matters is the fabric of associations, each case, however insignificant and routine, contributes to perpetuating and developing its meshes. This is another way of interpreting what Gabriel Tarde intimates when he explains that law always seeks to extend, never to shrink: he does not mean to say that law seeks to meddle in ever more things but on the contrary that, within its restricted domains, it seeks only to densify ever more: a densification, thus, as much in extension as in intension.

31 Case II   Ronald Dworkin once distinguished between 'hard cases' and 'easy cases' in judicial practice.[11] Yet from the point of view of a practice that takes cases as its exclusive objects, this distinction is grotesque. Distinguishing between 'easy' cases that require of judges the implementation of their most ingrained practical routines and 'hard' cases that on the contrary require profound reflection that can go all the way to the 'principles of justice' that found their functioning is absurd and vulgar. It is absurd because all cases are difficult, especially the most banal ones: all require treasures of invention to succeed in never needing the 'principles of justice'. And it is vulgar because, once again, the invocation of principles of justice re-stages the scene of incompetence that modern natural law had ridiculed in classical natural law. Theories like Ronald Dworkin's are manifestly philosophers' theories, not jurists' theories: from the point of view of the practice of law, in any case its topical practice, all they testify to is malice towards law. All of the difficulty of associationism, and all of its merit, consists precisely in working without anything that might be something other than an association, just as chain-smiths are quite uninterested in the principles of physics that govern the solidity of the chains they forge. For practitioners of law, it is about constructing a chain mail – but a chain mail not meant for anybody: not an 'inscribing socius', nor a despotic, a feudal, or a capitalist one (*AO*). Just as the topical practice of law seeks to be indifferent to the Law, to politics, and to economics, it seeks to be indifferent to all other forms of justice besides the ones contained in what we might call 'plastic' principles (*NP*, 50).

32 Jurisprudence   The topical practice of law is in fact no longer a practice of legislation, the way axiomatic practice is: it is a practice of *jurisprudence*. That is to say that the great inventions are no longer those that provide societies, individuals, or acts with a becoming but those that provide juridical operations with a becoming: associations seen from the technical point of view. Jurisprudence, in fact, is a historical taxonomy of cases: jurisprudence draws up the map of the extension of operations of association by which the practice of law proceeds towards its proper becoming. In the *Abécédaire*, Deleuze describes the privilege he confers on jurisprudence, a privilege that distinguishes it from the practice of legislators or lawyers. He takes the example of the prohibition to smoke in taxis. Deleuze describes this prohibition as undergoing two phases. In a first phase, this prohibition is the object of a fight based on location: a taxi cab is associated with a rented property, of which the renter enjoys 'customary right of support'. But in a second phase, matters are reversed: the taxi no longer constitutes a rented property but a public offer of service, of which the one using it cannot freely dispose. This evolution, and the little judicial battle that presides over it, in Deleuze's view forms a great example of jurisprudential practice: an evolution required by a situation which gives rise to a case through which the activity of creating law can exercise itself. But it is this activity, Deleuze explains, that is the most revolutionary: indifferent to Laws, to principles of justice and to institutions, jurisprudence is accountable only to the life whose juridical expression it is. Jurisprudence is life: this could be the principal slogan of Deleuze's philosophy of law (*A*, G).[12]

33 Principles   Yet even if jurisprudence possesses the anarchical spontaneity of life, it is not for all that without *principles*: its anarchism is a crowned anarchism. Thus, when

Nietzsche invokes 'plastic' principles, he is in reality singing the praises of a generalised jurisprudence. Jurisprudence experiments with the invention of principles that present the *three traits* Nietzsche calls for. The first trait is a demand concerning size: a principle must not be larger than what it conditions. The second trait is a demand concerning becoming: a principle must metamorphose along with what it conditions. The third trait is a demand concerning signification: a principle in each case is determined only along with what it determines. There is no principle worthy of the name that does not embrace that of which it constitutes the principle, that does not plastically follow its forms, trajectories and ramifications (*NP*, 50). In the thinking of the Law, principles always come first: they possess all they need even before a first case soliciting them comes along. In jurisprudence, on the contrary, the principles come last, if they ever come: it is the cases that give them their form, their content, and their signification. Yet in that sense, there are as many principles as there are cases, as many forms of principles as there are forms of cases, and so on. Principles are not some kind of precept starting from which one could attempt the systematic exploration of the diversity of accidents the practice of law encounters. We don't need microscopes, Deleuze says, talking about Proust, but telescopes: devices that enlarge what is far away rather than what is close (*PS*, 81–2). And it is from the very small that we think big rather than the other way around: the microscope brings the stars to us the way cases cut principles to match our size.

34 Leibniz In *The Fold*, Deleuze adds to the general privilege he grants jurisprudence a second privilege that places the topical practice of law above its axiomatic practice. The task, he explains, is in fact no longer only to think the practice of law in relation to a thinking of the Law that, in any event, has never had the slightest importance. The task is above all to proceed to a transformation of this practice itself that, if we follow Leibniz, would have to take the form of the metamorphosis of law into a 'universal Jurisprudence' (*FLB*, 77).[13] Yet it is precisely this metamorphosis that the most ordinary jurisprudence actualises every day when it looks into the cases submitted to it. The local problems of philosophy must be replaced with a general perplexity, without concept and without problem but made up of principles and cases. The – baroque – programme of this universal jurisprudence is as follows:

> [W]e shall multiply principles – we can always slip a new one out from under our cuffs – and in this way we will change their use. We will not have to ask what available object corresponds to a given luminous principle, but what hidden principle responds to whatever object is given, that is to say, to this or that 'perplexing case'. Principles as such will be put to a reflective use. A case being given, we shall invent its principle. It is a transformation from Law to universal Jurisprudence.
>
> We witness the honeymoon of singularity and the concept. (*FLB*, 76–7)

In actualising every day the programme of universal Jurisprudence, the topical practice of law not only proclaims its independence vis-à-vis the thinking of the Law, that is to say, vis-à-vis philosophy. It also gives philosophy a new horizon that could upend it. It is the great paradox of the topical practice of law that it forces philosophy into a marriage whose wedding philosophy, for its part, celebrated around the year zero.

35 Rome   It has become banal to oppose the speculative force of the Greeks to the pragmatic coarseness of the Romans: the ones a people of philosophers, the others a people of jurists. It has become even more banal, in taking up this opposition, to assert the greatness of the Greeks, who rose all the way to thinking, over against Roman stupidity, incapable of seeing further than the tip of its case. Yet in Nietzsche, there is an entirely different point of view on this question. What if it was the Greeks who were the calamity, a calamity that the Romans tried to *repair* as best they could? What if Roman pragmatism was a way to respond to the stupidity embodied by the Greek speculations? In his own way, Deleuze takes up Nietzsche's questions. When he speaks of law, something like a watchword transpires: we must stop being Greeks; we must become Romans once more. What is practising law the way one does philosophy good for, anyway? Why poison it again with philosophy, since the everyday practice of law, the practice of jurisprudence, is the freest practice? But becoming Roman again means not only recovering a form of technical purity of law. It also means recovering a form of technical purity of philosophy: the genius of law, because it is exclusively practical, is to actualise what philosophy must set as its horizon. Becoming Roman once more, in consequence, means this, an astonishing proposition: law is the future of philosophy. Because the practice of law is independent from all that philosophy must rid itself of in order finally to implement the programme of transcendental empiricism that Deleuze assigns to it, it embodies the first and most complete success of this programme. All that remains for philosophy is to step back and meditate on its failures: the sciences, arts, politics – and thinking.

36 Existence That jurisprudence is the philosophy of law and that it proceeds via singularity, as extending singularities, must be understood as follows. (a) Jurisprudence is the future of philosophy because it actualises the programme of philosophy. (b) This programme consists in the replacement of the Law and of problems with principles and cases. (c) The actualisation of this programme has always already taken place since jurisprudence has always been a casuistics and the place where new principles have been invented. (d) The origin of this actualisation lies in the fact that law has never left the age of its topical practice. (e) The axiomatic practice of law is not a juridical practice but a philosophical practice. From these five points of view, Deleuze is concerned with setting up a clinic of law: with establishing a map of law's possible modes of existence and of these different modes' respective

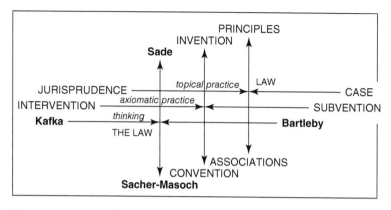

Figure 6 Diagram of the practice of law

values. Point by point, a clinic of the practice of law corresponds to the thinking of the Law, a clinic that increasingly detaches from what law was attached to for too long. In this sense, the clinic of the practice of law that Deleuze attempts must be seen as an endeavour to seek out and find what we might call the 'false problems' of law. These false problems are not only those of the Law but, ultimately, also those that constitute the axiomatic practice of law: legalism, naturalism, consensualism, and institutionalism – *in their two versions*. The issue is to establish jurisprudence as a practice whose autonomy consists in creating disjunctive relationships with everything around it, in 'construct[ing] *revolutionary connections* in opposition to the *conjugations of the axiomatic*' (*TP*, 473, Deleuze and Guattari's emphases).

Notes

1. See 'Postscript on Control Societies', *N*, 177–82; 'On Four Poetic Formulas that Might Summarise the Kantian Philosophy', *ECC*, 27–35, here 33; and *WP*, 106–10.
2. Sloterdijk, *Critique of Cynical Reason*, 229–50.
3. For instance, in *What is Philosophy?*: 'A great deal of innocence or cunning is needed by a philosophy of communication that claims to restore the society of friends, or even of wise

men, by forming a universal opinion as "consensus" able to moralise nations, States, and the market' (*WP*, 107).

In 'G comme gauche': 'All that respect for human rights, it's . . . you're tempted . . . to say nasty things . . . It's so much part of that flabby thinking . . . of that impoverished period we were talking about. It's . . . pure abstraction.' Or again: 'You say human rights. But that's a discourse for intellectuals, odious intellectuals, intellectuals that don't have ideas.' And even: 'Really, they're morons. Or, worse, I think, they're . . . hypocrites, all that thinking of human rights. Worthless, philosophically it's worthless' (*A*, G).

And in *Foucault*: 'This is not the first time an idea has been called eternal in order to mask the fact that it is actually weak or summary and is not even aware of those elements that might sustain it' (*F*, 90).

4. Zourabichvili, *The Vocabulary of Deleuze*, 197 (quoting *LS* 83) and 170 [modified].
5. See Foucault, 'Le grand enfermement', as well as *Discipline and Punish*.
6. See Tarde, *Les transformations du droit*, 76.
7. Tarde, *Les transformations du droit*, 147.
8. See Schmitt, *The* Nomos *of the Earth*; see also Guillaume Sibertin-Blanc's commentary in *Politique et État*, 84–102.
9. See *ES*, 132: 'The fact is that associationism is the theory of all that is practice, action, morality, and law.'
10. See Latour, *The Making of Law*.
11. See Dworkin, *Law's Empire*, 353–4.
12. The case Deleuze describes is fictitious. But it is a useful fiction because it dramatises an opposition more effectively than any theory ever could. Edward Mussawir has tried to construct a way of using this notion of dramatisation in *Jurisdiction in Deleuze*.
13. In his eponymous book, Patrick Riley has set out to reconstruct 'Leibniz' universal jurisprudence'. See also de Sutter and McGee, 'Postscript'.

Conclusion

1 *Personae*   At bottom, Deleuze's philosophy of law is not so much a philosophy as it is the admission of a regret: the regret that philosophy is less *advanced* than law. Philosophy must still rid itself of that Law to which law, in itself, grants no importance whatsoever. In placing Nietzsche's wish to be done with judgement at the heart of his thinking, Deleuze addresses philosophy more than law. In *Dialogues*, he seems to have harsh words for judges: 'Better to be a road-sweeper than a judge' (D, 8). But in *Nietzsche and Philosophy*, he specifies which judge he is talking about: the 'justice of the peace' as the conceptual persona that embodies all the stupidity of critique in the Kantian sense. The justice of the peace is the one who believes himself to be overturning truth or morality but forgets that it is morality and truth themselves we need to get rid of (*NP*, 90). Deleuze opposes this justice of the peace to the legislator as the one true inventor, a figure he discovers in Hume and which Nietzsche elaborates as well. If thinking is judging, then judging is equivalent to creating values rather than preventing their development, and that is what the legislator does (*NP*, 94). Yet these are still conceptual personae: the judge, the legislator, but also the lawyer or the investigator, are so many faces of philosophy. As such, they are distinct from the practitioners of legislation or of jurisprudence: they are content with embodying juridical traits proper to the philosophical concept when it becomes an adventure rather than a sanction. Thus, the judge of Kant's tribunal is opposed by Hume's investigator, Nietzsche's legislator, and Leibniz's lawyer (*WP*, 72). Yet even if they are conceptual personae, these different faces of judgement say

something about the profound, conflictual relationship that philosophy entertains with law.

2 Judgement   The ultimate goal that Deleuze, like Nietzsche, assigns to philosophy is to be done with judgement. Rather than judge, that is to say, critique, it is better to investigate, describe, and invent: we must go from a negative conception of philosophy to a positive one. It is precisely this positivity without remainder that Deleuze perceives in law in general and in jurisprudence in particular. It may well be a practice that contributes to the subjection of those who respect it, but law does not operate this subjection. There is an innocence of law that derives from the fact that it is stranger to judgement. A judge only ever settles. We must be done with the voluntarism we find in all decisionisms: in settling, nothing is decided since the real issue is to invent something new. Because it implies a practice stranger to judgement, law is never guilty of anything except, sometimes, a deficit of invention. It happens that the reactive forces seeking to seize it triumph and that the jurists' active forces are annulled in politics, economics, or science. But those are not the defeats Deleuze is interested in: his philosophy of law is a praise of juridical practice. And perhaps it is the only true praise of this practice in the entire history of thinking, since it is a praise that finds all of its arguments in law itself. The innocence of law has something autistic about it, but of the smiling autism of Proust's or Lewis Carroll's young girls, against whom all attempts at restoring the sinister prestige of the Law come up short and make fools of themselves. Being done with judgement, for philosophers, might be just this: becoming young girls sitting in a tribunal composed of playing cards and becoming so big that the game can no longer be played.

3 Errors   There is, however, an error to avoid. The praise of the practice of law Deleuze constructs is not a praise of the activity of courts and tribunals. We must distinguish between practice in the speculative sense and practice in the sociological sense. Unlike sociologists, Deleuze is indifferent to the social determinations of law: he holds that law knows nothing of them. There is a second error not to commit. That Deleuze is interested in law only from the angle of its essence does not mean that he aims, the way Hans Kelsen did, at constructing a pure theory of law. Nothing could be more impure. Against Kelsen, who believes that norms form the totality of law and whom he never mentions, Deleuze holds that norms, like sanctions, are nothing in law. The practice of law is a practice of inventing mechanisms of association that pick up on each other: law is a Meccano set. Nothing could be more foreign to this astonishing map of juridical operations than the ideas of norm and sanction. In the idea of a norm, invention is once more banished in favour of repetition; and in the idea of sanction, the multiplication of principles is reduced to a function of punishment. Deleuze's philosophy of law aims to establish a concept of jurisprudence that can serve as a gear between law and philosophy. But it is a concept for philosophical use since jurisprudence is without concept (all it has is operations). In a certain way, Deleuze's philosophy of law is without any utility for jurists. And, in a different way, it is of infinite utility because it allows for returning to the operations of law otherwise than if they were the expression of the Law.

4 Continuations   Deleuze's philosophy of law seems as solitary as a rare diamond. And yet some have crossed the path it has opened up. The most important among these, perhaps, are Bruno Latour and Isabelle Stengers. In *The Making of Law*, Latour shows how much law is a fabric without signification and without value. And at the same time, he shows that its signification and its value come precisely from their absence. He also shows how much jurists prove to be indifferent to everything in law that is not operation. And he shows, finally, to what extent these operations are of the order of invention rather than of conservation or policing.[1] Similarly, Stengers, in a number of articles and interviews, shows how much law indeed pertains to a regime of practice. But she also shows that this practice is speculative: it is a practice whose obligations and demands are not limited to those of corporatism. It is the operations of law themselves that demand of those who invent them that they prove their respect for them. She equally shows to what extent justice is stranger to law except in the form of a category of judgement that qualifies a successful juridical invention. And she shows, finally, to what extent the criterion for evaluating the judiciary is hesitation: in law, invention is not of the order of sudden illumination but of slow rumination.[2] Bruno Latour and Isabelle Stengers thus pursue the public health work begun by Deleuze with his wish to rid law of the false problems encumbering it. Some have responded to this work by saying that these are banalities from which jurists have nothing to learn. But they fail to understand that in fact philosophy has nothing to teach jurists other than the fact that it has nothing to teach them. In the world of jurists as in the Matrix, ignorance is bliss.

5 Politics   Some have reproached Deleuze's philosophy with the same thing that James's philosophy was reproached with in its day: with being a philosophy of the zeitgeist, that is to say, a philosophy of conformism. Yet this reproach is both moronic and idiotic. It is moronic from the point of view of understanding because nothing is more foreign to Deleuze's philosophy than the problem of conformism and revolt. To oppose conformism and revolt is to understand nothing about either one. There are some fierce pages in Deleuze on transgression and its interpretation by Bataille: Deleuze was anti-conformist in the sense that he loathed transgression (e.g. *D*, 47). But it is also an idiotic reproach from the point of view of the intellect because it amounts to considering that all those who choose to live in conformism are wrong to do so. Once again, this restages the scene of judgement and of error: conformism is an error that the judgement of conformism aims to reveal. Whereas for Deleuze, as for James, the concern is to show the beauties not of ordinary life but of the fact that life is never ordinary. When he brings his philosophy of law to an end by pointing to the parallel between life and jurisprudence, Deleuze insists on the inventive forces at work in both. These inventive forces, however, are inventive precisely thanks to a conformism that borders on asceticism: it is so easy to distinguish oneself, to be different. How much more difficult it is, by contrast, to be absolutely similar, to become impersonal! We must thus understand Deleuze's philosophy of law as a leftist philosophy in the sense suggested by Deleuze himself: in the sense of conformist asceticism. Being leftist is not only to sympathise and to shout, it is also to invent unheard-of operations, to refuse the judgement that condemns and the Law that elects.

6 Deception According to Deleuze, the subtle pleasure of deceiving is one of philosophy's greatest joys, just as saddening ought to be its goal: deceiving the dreamers fighting against the possibility that dreams must above all be lived, and saddening those who consider that the way the world goes ought to be a source of rejoicing or on the contrary of tears. Just as there is in Deleuze a political ascetism and just as there is a stylistic dryness to his writing, as Clément Rosset has stressed, there is a harshness to his thinking.[3] Deleuze's philosophy of law is a cruel philosophy, a philosophy without psychoactive drugs. The Law, justice, the social contract, they are all drugs that philosophers like to abuse as do those who in their wake wish for the good of humanity. But the Machiavellianism of terror, of force, or of violence are drugs just as much, abused this time by those who would like to consider humanity a waste. For Deleuze, humanity is not worth the trouble of being considered a waste or a treasure: what interests him is not humanity but the way in which individuals organise to compose societies, to elaborate relations and to ensure the robustness of the acts they posit. In this sense, Deleuze's philosophy of law is not a humanist philosophy: on the contrary, it is a nihilist philosophy, provided we remember that Nietzsche distinguished between at least two kinds of nihilism. There is the passive nihilism of those constantly haunted by their bad conscience: this, precisely, is the nihilism of the friends of the Law. And then there is an active nihilism, which is the nihilism of those who do not want to enter into any compromise with life because life itself is without compromise (*NP*, 147–52). These latter nihilists are the great creators. And jurists, perhaps, are the greatest among them.

Notes

1. See Latour, *The Making of Law* and 'Note brève', as well as the comments by Serge Gutwirth and myself in 'Droit et cosmopolitique'. Latour responds in the introduction to the English translation of *The Making of Law*. For a first attempt at an interpretation, see Saunders, 'Cases against Transcendence', as well as Kyle McGee's important book, *Bruno Latour: The Normativity of Networks*.
2. See Stengers, 'Une pratique cosmopolitique du droit est-elle possible?' and *La Vierge et le neutrino*, 176–88.
3. See Rosset, 'Sécheresse de Deleuze'.

Appendices

1 The Young Girls in Deleuze's Philosophy of Law

1 Precursor   Between 1945 and 1947, Gilles Deleuze submitted five texts to several prestigious publications. Together, they form the first moment of his oeuvre – before the great silence that preceded the publication of *Empiricism and Subjectivity* in 1953. These were brilliant and singular texts that proved those right who, in the entourage of Marie-Madeleine Davy, Deleuze's mentor during the Occupation, saw in him a 'new Sartre', despite his young age.[1] Later, however, he decided to take them off his bibliography and even to prohibit any republication or collection, including after his death. These texts were refused acknowledgement – as if Deleuze meant to say that they, too, belonged to the meditative silence that preceded his first true work: his first book. All in all, they could claim no other status than that of school exercises, rough drafts with no other goal than to serve as a training ground for the progressive development of concepts to come. When much later, in *What is Philosophy?*, Deleuze offers his famous definition of philosophy – it is the 'creation of concepts' – he no doubt remembers the labour of elaborating his own. It is this labour that he wants to see disappear in favour of a long interval of invisibility that could constitute the 'dark precursor' of his own thinking: the existence of his first texts was too *clear and distinct*. Even if the event of concept creation cannot be thought as a *fiat lux* but is already included in the fabric of the world, this inclusion must still be laid out. If the event does have a precursor, in turn, it has no rough draft: its perfection must already be whole in the precursor – the way the rhizome is wholly contained in the least of its shoots. This, perhaps, is the reason for Deleuze's disavowal of his first texts: because they had been published, they had become too actual, not virtual enough.

2 Surface   Deleuze's very first text – 'Description of Woman: For a Philosophy of the Sexed Other', published in *Poésie* in the autumn of 1945 – can serve as privileged testimony in establishing the reasons that pushed him to make the productions of his youth disappear. Since the publication two years earlier of *Being and Nothingness*, he had kept professing an increasing admiration for the work of Jean-Paul Sartre, as Michel Tournier recounts in *The Wind Spirit*. When Deleuze discovered Sartre's book, Tournier explains, he called him every day on the phone to tell him about the enthusiastic observations that arose from the progress of his reading. But later, not long after the Liberation, at the moment that Sartre's celebrity exploded everywhere, the deception was as great as the earlier infatuation had been: *Sartre was a humanist after all*. In the meantime, 'Description of Woman' appeared, which sees itself as an addendum to the chapters on desire and sexuality in *Being and Nothingness* and at the same time as a way of taking up a reproach that Sartre addresses to Heidegger. The reproach is that Heidegger's philosophy has led only to sketching an unsexed humanity – when in reality sexuality is the cause of everything. In 'Description of Woman', Deleuze thus tries to endow the forgotten figure of woman with a 'philosophical status' whose principal traits he articulates in keeping with the terms of Sartre's thinking (17). Yet even if it is something of a 'pastiche' (as François Dosse has pointed out),[2] Deleuze's article already manifests several obsessions we find in his 'acknowledged' works. And the first of these is a predilection for surfaces: what counts in woman, Deleuze explains, is above all make-up – that is to say, the way in which what would otherwise be but a blind interiority is given an artificial surface.

3 Interiority Because the issue is thinking this principal interiority of woman – as opposed to the just as principal exteriority of man – any theory of woman in the view of the young Deleuze must be a theory of make-up. To this end, he distinguishes between two great categories of cosmetics: the 'make-up of surfaces' (powders, ointments, rouge, and so on) and the 'make-up of orifices' (mascara, lipstick, and so on) (*DW*, 21). While the make-up of the first category allows for bringing out the surfaces of the face of woman, Deleuze explains, only that of the second category contributes, by highlighting the exterior, to revealing her fundamental interiority. To highlight the eyes or the mouth is to invite plunging into this interiority – that is to say, to experience its existence, which, he adds, is the very existence of the world:

> Woman is a concrete universal, she is a world – not an external world, but the underworld of the world, a tepid interiority of the world, a compress of the internalised world. Hence the prodigious sexual success of woman: to possess the woman is to possess the world (*DW*, 19).

In describing the two kinds of make-up and describing the woman in make-up as holding the secret to the interiority of the world, a secret accessible only via a cosmetic artifice, Deleuze reveals himself. He says a lot more about himself than the ethics of discretion he subsequently practises can accept: he speaks the above all cerebral character of his relation to sexuality and to woman. But he also speaks the pulsional truth that feeds all ideas of masks, make-up, cosmetics or simulacra – a truth articulated, this time, in terms that are *too* sexed to be admissible. Before he even begins to elaborate the theory of desire whose cosmic accents will make him famous, his actual truth is already made visible to all: *there can be no other desire than that of a man for a woman in make-up.*

4 Perturbation In Deleuze's later work, the fascination with the figure of woman takes a more discrete and more complicated turn – woman as such no longer appears explicitly. In turn, as Catherine Backès-Clément (who is the only one to have noticed this) remarks, another persona begins to assume an increasingly considerable place: the *young girl*.[3] From *Coldness and Cruelty* to *Kafka*, from *Proust and Signs* to *Logic of Sense*, young girls begin to proliferate in Deleuze's work as so many anamorphoses of the forgotten woman. While there is no longer any question of make-up or even of interiority, the young girl occupies a strange place in his system: that of the *perturbing other*. The young girl is the element whose presence entails the impossibility for any order – whatever it may be, though most often, its agents are fathers and mothers – to one day enjoy the comfort of its own closure. In Deleuzian vocabulary, the young girls represent so many 'lines of flight' by which what claims to be contained in the interior of an order reveals a dimension irreducible to this claim. The most striking example is the role that sisters, maids, and whores (three different forms of young girls) play in Kafka's work as read jointly by Deleuze and Guattari (*K*, 65–6). The machinery of the Law in which the protagonists of Kafka's novels are caught up keeps revealing vacuoles that escape it – vacuoles of the Law's *craze* where the Law has no say. This craze that the young girls inflict on Kafka's figures is also the one that Lewis Carroll's Alice produces in the queen's croquet game or the one that groups of adolescents cause in the obsessional narrator of *In Search of Lost Time*. In all these cases, a regulated state of affairs is confronted with a reality stronger than its will to regulation can contain: the *reality of desire*.

5 Disturbance   In going from woman to young girl, Deleuze at first does nothing more than go from the concrete reality of this desire – 'to possess the woman is to possess the world' – to a more abstract and thus more euphemised reality. Desire, the pulsional truth of a positive idea of woman, becomes the pure concept of a negative idea of the same woman – the young girl, in opposition to the mother, basically being *woman as woman in make-up*. Where as positive idea, woman gives access to the interiority of the world, as negative idea, she refuses men the satisfaction of definitively settling in the order of exteriority that is theirs. Yet this passage from the concrete to the abstract or from the positive to the negative does not take place without a price being paid: dividing the world of women into two unequal sections. With the figure of the young girl, access to the interiority of the world (or the disruption of the comfort of settling in a pure exteriority) stops being a possibility open to all women. Only young girls, as *women in make-up*, can henceforth claim to offer this access – while the other women, as *not in make-up*, are confined in the same exteriority as men. Or, rather: are deprived of the interiority constitutive of them, such that their presence in the world of exteriority suddenly has no other thickness than that of a ghost or spectre. Just as for the young Deleuze make-up is the source of the desire prompted by the experience of interiority offered by women, so for the mature Deleuze this source is to be found only in young girls. A sort of imbalance is thus introduced into the group of women: the ability to offer this experience of interiority is reserved to one subgroup. Yet this experience is modified by the imbalance as well: the experience of interiority no longer entails a reconciliation with the world – it has become a disturbance.

6 *Tekhnē* Deleuze never describes, in a systematic way, the disturbance of the order of the world introduced by the figure of the young girl – although, as noted, it is a recurrent figure. The revolutionary force inherent to the desire prompted by the young girl undoubtedly seems to him an explanatory factor precise enough to be able to dispense with any further elaboration. For Deleuze, the question of the young girl can be solved in the question of the desire she provokes – that is to say, fundamentally, in the Spinozism of the event that still today is associated with her name. Nonetheless, the singular relation that the young girl and desire entertain in his work would have merited asking the question that, according to

Deleuze himself, is the most important question: *how?* That is to say, how does the young girl go about prompting, through the desire she gives rise to, a disturbance in the order of the world – a 'line of flight' interior to its exteriority? That the question of desire is associated in a privileged way with what Deleuze calls a 'conceptual persona' signals the implication of something pertaining to a *drama*. Desire is not only a matter of event and becoming: it is a matter of *plotting* event and becoming – a matter of constructing or creating them. *How does one create disorder?* is the question posed by the figure of the young girl in Deleuze's work – a question the concept of desire, as such, does not solve. To begin answering it, it would indeed have been necessary to reread 'Description of Woman' – which would amount, for Deleuze, to reconciling himself with his own Sartrean past, even with his own desires. The answer would then have appeared, bright as day: to create disorder, all it takes is a very simple gesture, a gesture that, because it is very simple, is impossible to circumvent – all it takes is *to take out one's lipstick*. Cosmetics is the very *tekhnē* of disorder.

7 Obscenity   Perhaps I should give an example of the *cosmetics of the event* of which Deleuze, because of his strange obsession with young girls, makes himself, *nolens volens*, the silent advocate. In *Kafka*, he and Guattari devote significant effort to establishing the validity of a theorem that might seem extravagant: the theorem according to which the Law is written 'in a porno book' (*K*, 49). In their view, this theorem must above all be taken to enounce the reality it claims to describe: the judges' library in the *Trial* contains nothing but obscene volumes. Yet beyond this description, it suggests that the reality thus described is obscene on another level as well, a level we may call 'critical' provided we use the term in the specific way Deleuze uses it. To say that the Law is written in a porno book is in fact to highlight that in staging the judges as readers of obscene literature, Kafka's work seeks to say something about *the Law itself*. That is to say, the fact that the books consulted by the judges in their hearings are not strangers to their function but, on the contrary, are those most appropriate to it. If, taken together, the books read by the judges can be said to constitute a gigantic 'porno book', it is because they are indeed *books of Law* – or, rather, *the very book of the Law*. Yet since the obscenity of the scenes described by these books has to do with the obscenity of what is taking place behind the scenes of the court, an ambiguity enters into Deleuze and Guattari's theorem. What is the difference between the descriptions that figure in the book of the Law and the moments of craze experienced by Josef K. in the company of maids, young girls, and whores? What is the difference between the *pornographic order of the Law* and the disorder that, according to the hypothesis Deleuze puts forward elsewhere, young girls are supposed to introduce to it? Could this be merely the fact that in the first case, it is just *images*?

8 Phantasm I   That an image can be qualified as 'porno' or, more widely, that it can give rise to desire, is among the possibilities Deleuze leaves aside – all the way to his books on cinema. He barely allows himself to point out, in an interview from 1985 and thus after the publication of *The Time-Image*, the decerebrate character of 'most cinematic production, with its arbitrary violence and feeble eroticism' (N, 60). Once again, the question of eroticism – as a category of the explication of the desire animating images – is grafted onto the question of cerebrality and of the image disconnected from all imaginary. Moreover, in his answers to a questionnaire submitted to him around the same time by a cinema journal, Deleuze does not hesitate to admit that he does not 'attach much importance to the notion of the imaginary' (N, 66). This explains why the notion of phantasm, which Lacanian psychoanalysis associates with that of the imaginary, is notably absent from Deleuze's philosophy of the image. In his thinking, there is no phantasm: all there is are realities – whose modalities, for all their variability, no less manifest their general, even absolute, character. Yet because it is an absolute realism, Deleuze's thinking is embarrassed by the young girls that keep cropping up and keep prompting the phantasms of those whose paths they cross – beginning with Deleuze himself. It is of course possible to speak of 'feeble eroticism' in the case of the pornographic images with which Kafka's judges regale themselves, but what about the offers the whores make? Are they not 'images', too – and thus a 'reality' that can claim a type of status equivalent to that of other images, 'porno' or not? Deleuze is never clear on this point: his predilection for cerebrality keeps him from seeing that phantasms, like all things, can be said to be *real*.

9 *Phantasms II* If, as Deleuze and Guattari say, the order of the Law is founded on a 'porno book', we must conclude that the disorder of this order is so just as much – that is to say, porn is the *centre* of the Law. Porn is that which, at the centre of the Law, *orders the disorder*: it is the operation by which the Law reveals, simultaneously, its phantasmic power and, through this phantasm, its real powerlessness. In this sense, the cosmetics of the event whose terms Deleuze suggests in 'Description of Woman' is indeed a realism of phantasm. The concrete phantasm prompted by the young girl *is* the operator that introduces into the Law an *interior outside* by which the comfort of its 'exteriority' is immediately annihilated – or, rather: crazed. This operator of craze, while cerebral, is obviously cerebral in the decerebrate sense of 'feeble eroticism' – and thus also of the 'imaginary' constituted by the phantasm that activates it. When they write that 'the Law is written in a porno book', Deleuze and Guattari suggest, despite themselves, that the Law, more so than a book, is an image – even, beyond the single image, a *film*. The film of phantasms prompted by the young girls is the medium through which the operation that results in the crazing of the order of the Law deploys and effects itself as that which makes this very order possible. *The reality of the order of the Law is the reality of the pornographic phantasms prompted*

by the young girls – that is to say, by women as women in make-up, since make-up is what gives body to the phantasm of interiority. We might thus summarise the entire ambiguity of the role played by the young girls in Deleuze by saying that in his thinking, they are the embodiment of the desire that gives rise to an event *insofar as they are the embodiment of phantasms that give rise to disorder.* Through them, however, this ambiguity extends well beyond their proper reality: it manages to contaminate every image.

10 Viewer   Like all philosophers of his generation, Deleuze keeps claiming to dismiss the subject from the landscape of thinking; yet, also like them, he keeps seeing it come back, in his work, in places from which he thought he had evacuated it.[4] In the case of Deleuze's philosophy of cinema, this phenomenon, though more subtle there than elsewhere, has entailed the same consequence: the phantom-like return of the *viewer*. When Jacques Rancière claims that Deleuze's philosophy of cinema is the philosophy of nothing but itself (and thus certainly not of cinema), he, too, is mistaken about this return.[5] In claiming to establish a natural history of cinema, whose different branches would designate so many species of images, Deleuze's explicit agenda is indeed to reinvent the concept of time. But this reinvention is inscribed within the frame of a history of cinema that may lead us to think that only films (and even: only 'great' films) are able to provide the *experience* of time. Deleuze's philosophy of cinema, in this sense, is much closer to phenomenology than any of his other writings – since what he proposes there is an *aesthetics of the reception of time*. The images of cinema, as the main medium of the different forms of time, are unthinkable without at least one viewer who is able to establish their exhaustive catalogue: Deleuze himself – and thus not just anybody. This makes it easier to understand why the 'feeble eroticism' he talks about in the interview on *The Time-Image* does not have a positive counterpart in this catalogue. For Deleuze, eroticism is always 'feeble' in that it replaces the pure cerebrality of the thinking of time with another, impure cerebrality: that of the phantasmatic experience of images. Since, on the one hand, eroticism is always 'feeble' and, on the other, all experience is that of a subject prey to phantasms, the conclusion imposes itself all on its own: *all experience is feeble – and thus erotic.*

11 Image   Deleuze needed to suppress himself as a viewer of cinema in order to constitute images as pure forms of the concept of time and to forget the phantasm that led him there in the first place. He needed to dismiss the experience of images and, through it, the singular erotic experience of the viewer in order for the young girls traversing the cinema to be put back in a place where they no longer represent any danger. In claiming to deploy a system of time via the examination of the different forms of images that time could adopt, Deleuze is very much concerned with conjuring a danger. This danger is the reappearance of 'Description of Woman' and thus also of the 'humanism' for which he and Tournier had so much reproached their teacher Sartre at the time. At bottom, Deleuze, like Sartre, fails to leave humanism behind – quite simply because, like Sartre, he continues to desire in the most banal, the least Spinozist way possible. When we reread his 'Description of Woman' and compare it with the figures of young girls appearing elsewhere in his work, we must realise that the praise of make-up we find there is a praise of *images.* More exactly, it is a praise of girl-images – that is to say, of girls to be found in magazines to whom make-up gives a singular reality. The catalogue of the different kinds of images that Deleuze sets out to write in his books on cinema is the cerebral form of the catalogue of different kinds of girls. When he describes these girls as the source of the craze of the order of the Law, we must understand that they are above all a source of craze for *him* – for the philosophical order he is trying to build. They are the persistent mark of the cerebral phantasm that pushed him to find in the concept a world where the force of desire can finally be expressed in full freedom.

12 Outside   Once 'Description of Woman' turns out to be the hidden key to Deleuze's relationship to both images and women, it becomes possible to understand how necessary it was for him to repudiate it. And in truth, this repudiation went a long way: it took with it the possibility of an outside of philosophy – a province of the world where the concept is not the only admissible entity. Just as the young girls are smuggled into Deleuze's work, so this outside sometimes returns there, in the most unexpected form. This form is the form of law. Be it in his conversations with Claire Parnet, in *Thousand Plateaus*, or in *Coldness and Cruelty*, law in Deleuze shares with the young girls a spectral status. The reason for this shared status is clear albeit, no doubt, unexpected: *the young girls and law are, in reality, one and the same thing.* In the same way as the young girls, law in Deleuze intervenes only to *disturb* the comfortable order of the Law, this order whose herald philosophy understood itself to be. Law is the place where the Law fails to conclude its exteriority: the place where the Law's internal outside appears, the exteriority of exteriority, the practice of its concept. The Law, heritage of the Greek philosophy of the *logos*, is what law, heritage of the Roman practice of *ius*, keeps driving crazy when it manifests the impossibility of the Law's claims, whatever they be. In *Coldness and Cruelty*, this opposition is clear: the 'images of the Law' traversing the history of philosophy (Plato or Kant) are opposed by so many critiques of these images (CC, 81–90). Yet these critiques are themselves but the first moment of a much more radical crazing of the system of the Law, a purely negative moment that must be followed by a positive moment. The negative moment is that of philosophical critique; the positive moment that of juridical clinic.

13 Philosophy   This may have been the source of Deleuze's discomfort: because it keeps on dismissing the possibility of an outside of the concept (of an outside of the cerebral), philosophy remains grafted onto a thinking of the Law. As the young girls come in to craze, by the phantasms they prompt, the cerebral order of desire, they must be ejected from this order, just as the practice of law must be presented as antagonistic to philosophy. But since Deleuze's philosophical attempt aims precisely to include once more in the order of philosophy what had been excluded from it, he needs the young girls just as he needs law. He needs them as much for structural reasons (establishing the possibility of an outside in philosophy) as for personal reasons (restoring the presence of his phantasm – which is inadmissible). That he never brings it up and even refuses the publication one day of the texts that allow for finding the reasons for it is one of the most embarrassing theoretical gestures of the past half-century. Giving the young girls and law a philosophical status, as antagonists of philosophy, would have been conceivable only if Deleuze had accepted the reality of phantasms and the necessity of the viewer. Because he decided, for reasons linked to the historical situation, to follow the movement of the critique of the imaginary and of the critique of the subject at work in his epoch, this possibility was foreclosed. Today, however, we may consider the true radicalness of his thinking to lie not in this *satisfecit* he granted the demands of his time but in the self-destruction of philosophy it proclaimed. This self-destruction is at the heart of his thinking, like a time bomb waiting to go off, since he himself, after planting it, preferred to place himself out of danger. Or, at least, he pretended to try escaping – which may well be another of his tricks.

14 Pornology   Despite his rejection of 'feeble eroticism', there is an expression of Deleuze's that we must recall: we need, he explains in *Coldness and Cruelty*, a new 'pornology' (*CC*, 18). This word, which shows up only in this one place, is not being developed specifically other than to designate the application of pornographic logic to philosophy. Like the concept 'simulacrum' in *Logic of Sense* or in *Difference and Repetition*, it is a kind of theoretical *hapax* that is abandoned as soon as it is pronounced, without being established in a decisive way. Once more, we may have to regard this almost immediate denial as the trace of an existentially irresistible temptation that philosophy's characteristic demands lead him to reject. Yet, as for the young girls and for law (or for simulacra – let's say: for images), this temptation seems to concern more than a simple intuition: it designates a veritable system. For Alain Badiou, all of Deleuze's philosophy must be considered a system in the sense that classical French philosophy – and that means above all, Descartes or Malebranche – has given the term.[6] If this is true, then we must add that Deleuze's philosophical system is doubled by a shadow: by a *counter-system* that keeps coming in to parasitise the perfection of the first system. Young girls, law, and images form the main coordinates of this counter-system, and it is not whimsical to think that the specific name of this counter-system is, precisely, 'pornology'. Pornology is the anti-philosophical gesture by which philosophy gives itself its own outside even as it keeps on doing everything for this outside to be declared impossible. We must thus establish the following equation: pornology = young girls + images + law. Deleuze kept mining his text with this explosive anti-philosophical equation, all the while refusing to activate it. He was his own traitor.

15 Theorems   It would take a lot of effort to reconstitute, in each of its parts, the anti-philosophical system proper to Deleuze's philosophy – and to render it the justice he refused it. As a kind of introduction, until somewhere, someday, this effort is made more consistently, we may content ourselves with recalling its most important utterances. There are three of them, and they form so many theorems as susceptible to demonstration as they are to illustration: the theorem of the young girl; the theorem of the image; and the theorem of law. The theorem of the young girl is: *every order prompts its own disorder, namely through the attempt at foreclosing its possibility* (what creates disorder is foreclosing the possibility of disorder). The theorem of the image is: *every reality prompts its own illimitation, namely through the attempt at excluding its opposite* (what establishes phantasms as reality proper is the refusal of phantasms). And the theorem of law is: *every Law prompts its own annulment, namely through the attempt at rationalising practice* (what annuls all possibility of Law is the affirmation of the supremacy of the Law). While it is difficult to articulate these three theorems in any other way than by rendering them equivalent – such that young girls, law, and images are but one and the same thing – we may still try. Let me therefore suggest this: since the young girl is what provokes in the Law the phantasms (the images) that disturb the cerebral regularity of its desire, she is the conceptual persona of which law is the practice. This can be put aphoristically: *law is the cosmetics of disorder* – and thus the vibration of law introduced into the interior of the abstract order of the Law. This lesson will undoubtedly seem disappointing, and one might consider that transforming law into the very embodiment of life is having a rather narrow (because libidinal) notion of life. That is possible. But since a wide notion of life is the object that the thinking of the Law has kept on giving itself, such a narrow notion alone will henceforth be able to *excite* us.

Notes

1. See Dosse, *Gilles Deleuze and Félix Guattari*, 92–8.
2. Dosse, *Gilles Deleuze and Félix Guattari*, 94.
3. Backès-Clément, 'Les Petites filles ou les aventures de la philosophie'.
4. On this point, see Žižek, *The Ticklish Subject*.
5. Rancière, 'The Indecisive Affect', 205–6. Alain Badiou makes the same mistake (*Deleuze*, 15–16).
6. See Badiou, *Deleuze*, 17.

2 On Some Interpretations of Deleuze's Philosophy of Law

1 Habit   Since this book was first published in French, the literature on Deleuze's philosophy of law has developed considerably. Alexandre Lefebvre was the first to produce a book on the subject, *The Image of Law: Deleuze, Bergson, Spinoza*, published by Stanford University Press in 2008. As its subtitle indicates, the book's ambition was to supplement what could appear to be an insufficiency in Deleuze's thinking by taking recourse to other thinkers. Or rather: the concern is to deploy, with the help of two of Deleuze's most important teachers, what in his work still takes a latent or not sufficiently affirmed form. With this gesture, Lefebvre posited what was to become the primary *habit* of the literature on Deleuze's juridical thinking, namely the expectation that this thinking *serve*. While this habit could appeal to the principle of betrayal I laid out in the introduction to the present work, it also had the consequence that Deleuze was never considered for himself. His thinking became a tool, and this or that argument or set of arguments, taken independently, could lead to this or that new lesson in matters of law. The ambition of this book, on the contrary, has been to produce a *full reconstruction* of Deleuze's philosophy of law. Starting with the collection of the totality of his declarations on the subject of law, my concern has been to present the most complete version possible of what (following Badiou) is commonly considered a *system*. From this point of view, the present work, modest though it is, remains, unfortunately, unique in its genre – which conditions its relationship with the other works produced in the same field.

2 Boundas I   In a review published in the spring 2011 issue of *Symposium*, Constantin Boundas was the first to suggest a relationship between this book and Lefebvre's.[1] His account favoured Lefebvre: it consisted in welcoming the fact that in his book, he developed a positive juridical invention starting from Deleuze's work. This invention was a philosophy of *rights* (and not of *law*) that allowed for getting out of what Boundas considers a general aporia at the heart of Deleuze's oeuvre – namely, its fleeting character. The argument, made in the past by Philippe Mengue, consists in reproaching Deleuze with not providing a *programme* in matters of politics (and thus in matters of law).[2] Since, as we saw in the second part, Deleuze's thinking is characterised by its involuntarism, such a programme could be nothing but the object of the most profound contempt in his eyes. For what is a programme if not, once again, the articulation of a set of decisions taken *before* any encounter with any kind of event – that is to say, before that which the programme is to guide? In Deleuzian terms, a programme is still Logos: a way of going back to the normative principle of things rather than being oriented by the very movement of their slow drift. Deleuze was neither reformist nor progressive – and if he was revolutionary, he was so in the Chinese rather than Jacobine way: revolution as *evolution*. Moreover, if he had a programme, it could never have been political (or juridical): his practice being the practice of philosophy, it could never have been anything but philosophical. And, rather than a programme to be implemented, it was more of an intuition to follow, the same way one follows a desire.

3 Boundas II   Boundas's favourable judgement of Lefebvre was thus based on the possibility of using Deleuze in a way that runs counter to his thinking. In fact, the principle of betrayal encouraged such an attitude – even if the quotation that serves as this book's epigraph implies that there are, undoubtedly, sad betrayals. Mengue's position has always been a sad one – it is the position of someone who looks for a teacher and, not finding one, turns against the one elected to take that place. In paying tribute to the programme of the philosophy of rights defended by Lefebvre, Boundas is going in a similar direction, looking for a *politics of law* where none exists. Addressing Lefebvre's book in his *Deleuzian Concepts*, Paul Patton, too, draws a similar hypothesis from it, delighted by what we might call its *liberal* character.[3] It is to be feared that here, we are as close as possible to the idea of a programme: not only is there a decision of principle but this decision pertains both to politics and to a certain politics. Yet if there is a politics of law that is a politics of rights, then for those who follow Deleuze literally, this politics cannot but pertain to the modern image of the Law: it is a politics of the Logos – a philosophical politics. *It is precisely against such a politics that Deleuze has constituted his philosophy of law*: it is the sworn enemy of law such as it constitutes the future of philosophy. In stressing the political character of Lefebvre's philosophy of rights, Boundas and Patton thus not only betray Deleuze, they betray him in the saddest way possible: by back-pedalling vis-à-vis what he tried with all his might to separate himself from.

4 Politics   We must add immediately that if there is no politics of law, that does not mean that law is without relation to politics – or that such relations would be inconsequential. The indifference of law towards politics is in fact a formal indifference: it is the indifference of someone who considers the decisions of the Logos to be given. Politics, on the contrary, because it is the site of *legislation*, of the concrete practice of the Logos of the Law, keeps producing new constraints that oblige the practitioners of the Nomos to come up with new creations. Bruno Latour and Isabelle Stengers have forcefully established just how weak the idea of a politics of law is from a political point of view – because it forgets both politics and law. Rather than of a politics of law ultimately determining the *quality* of its practice (which, ultimately, Mengue or Boundas are hoping for), we ought to speak of possible political uses of law. It is possible for law to contribute to the invention of a politics – but on the condition that the first moment of this invention not be its mutilation or contempt for it. Turning politics into the supreme determinant of law is precisely to operate such a mutilation of law, there where, if the idea is to betray Deleuze with humour (thus with joy), one would need to *enhance* it. In his afterword to the Italian edition of the present book, Sandro Chignola is aiming for just such an enhancement – as is Giso Amendola in a review of that translation published in *Il Manifesto*.[4] Only once Deleuze's involuntarism, his antinormativism, his critique, and his clinic have been accepted all the way can a political invention of law claim the status of a happy betrayal. For Chignola as for Amendola, this betrayal has a name, which as noted is neither reformism, nor progressivism, nor revolutionism but – *freedom*.

5 Lefebvre I In fact, the concept of freedom does not figure in Deleuze's oeuvre. He preferred instead to speak of 'crowned anarchy' (*DR*, 41), as if to insist that if there is freedom, it exists only insofar as it gives itself a constraint that can exceed those the Laws keep on articulating. It is thus in this context, rather than that of a 'politics of law', that we must understand Lefebvre's attempt at drawing a philosophy of rights from Deleuze. What he tries to circumscribe in *The Image of Law* are the operations by which it is possible to describe judges' creative activity *without* going back to the vocabulary of politics. He is very clear on this point: the idea is to be done with both the model of (political) *activism* and the model of (sociological) *accident* and to return to the observation of the 'everyday operation' of courts and tribunals.[5] As I wrote above, in judicial matters *nothing is more banal than creation* – and this banality, this everydayness of juridical invention is what needs to be accounted for in the most respectful manner. Nonetheless, Lefebvre's concern with practice quickly transforms into a concern with the activity of courts and tribunals such as it is – and such as it results in the granting (or refusal) of this or that specific right. The creation at issue in *The Image of Law* never includes the labour on the conditions in which and the constraints with which judges practise their activity. The orientation of this activity follows only one curve: a curve of invagination – but it never, it seems, turns towards an outside, following a curve of exfoliation. As in the reproach that Žižek aimed at Deleuze, everything there changes so that nothing changes – so that everything remains equal to itself.[6]

6 *Lefebvre II*   In a review of *The Image of Law*, Nathan Moore is more cruel, pointing the finger at the vocabulary of the 'image of thought' employed by Lefebvre.[7] In Deleuze's thinking of law, in fact, any image is an image of the Law demanding (and feeding in advance) its own critique – before prompting a subsequent clinic. That Lefebvre seeks to establish a new 'image' in juridical matters is all the more awkward for his not distinguishing between law and Law, as Deleuze does. The image of 'law' he suggests is an image that includes both the Law and law and refuses to acknowledge the *radical impossibility*, in the eyes of all practice of law, of an image of the Law – and be it in the weak form of its axiomatic practice. This reinforces the impression that the activity of creation to which he devotes his descriptive efforts is an immobile activity – or, at least, an activity at the mercy of the Logos or the compars. Even if it is not, as Boundas or Patton think, a matter of politics, something like a ghost of the Law keeps haunting Lefebvre's book, without it having much to say in reply. In return, Moore is unjust when he generalises the demand Deleuze articulates to be done with judgement and reproaches Lefebvre for still hewing to it. The judge, as conceptual persona, does indeed still pertain to philosophy; he has nothing to do with the practitioner of law whose activity consists in issuing rulings or decisions. It is only when the Law (in one or another of its images) triumphs that judges' judgements become forms of judgement in general – but this triumph is not what Lefebvre wants. While he does not want it, however, he has not defended himself more vigorously against the ghost of the Law, which leaves his work halfway on the path he had hoped to travel.

7 *Mussawir I*   Generally, the refusal to consider the difference between 'Law' and 'law' in Deleuze is a constant

source of awkwardness in his commentators. In his beautiful book, *Jurisdiction in Deleuze*, Edward Mussawir, too, does not mention it, contenting himself with highlighting the importance of jurisprudential practice in Deleuze's work. For Mussawir, it is another distinction of Deleuze's that needs to be looked at: that between 'representation' and 'expression', that is to say, between confirmation and creation. Rather than consider the practice of judges to be a practice of representation that sticks to applying a moral canon, we ought to perceive it as an activity that expresses a morality of its own. The great force of Mussawir's book is that it deploys this alternative by way of a series of technical examples concerning the figure of the subject of law, the problem of possession, or the question of procedure in law. In each of his examples, all based on multiple cases, Mussawir demonstrates the way in which judges are able to proceed to an invention of their own that owes nothing to others. The expressive dimension of jurisprudence, from this point of view, exceeds the dimension of simple morality and covers the totality of the layers of what we call reality. Because it is expressive rather than representative, the juridical genre is an irrealism: a genre for which reality (however defined) is but one constraint among others. If such is the consequence of Mussawir's investigation, we must still note that he does not articulate it in these terms: as in Lefebvre, the creative activity of judges seems, in Mussawir, just as enclosed as it was among the defenders of the representational genre.

8 Mussawir II   This sensation of enclosure is connected with the absence of any consideration of the difference that exists between 'Law' and 'law', and thus with the refusal to admit that *law is the outside*. The concrete reality of judiciary practice is what the Law is the representation of, while law is its comic *diversion* – that is, its true expressive dimension. There is in Mussawir, as in Lefebvre, Boundas, or Patton, a strange blindness when it comes to the *radicalness* of Deleuze's thinking of law, which, to repeat, is a radicalness that is entirely foreign to any politics. It is a radical thinking because the ontology it proffers no longer has anything to do with the Laws of Being or the Laws of the world – one that no longer has anything to do with any Law. The subject of law is thus a fiction that is not only operative but *liberating*: the subject liberates us (as Mussawir rightly detects) from the history of the subject *tout court*. In separating from the Law, law opens up infinite possibilities of lines of flight that no constraint, be it of morality, of politics, or even of realism, can close down. From this point of view, it can be argued that law is revolutionary: it is not beholden to anything that constitutes our world – *including law itself*. The danger in not differentiating between 'Law', understood in the very broad sense Deleuze gives it (as laid out at the end of the first part of this book), and 'law' is that under the cover of invention, creation, or expression, a kind of new juridical conservatism comes into being. To avoid it, there is only one task conceivable: to accept, all the way, that law is before everything else the everyday form taken, in our age, by science-fiction. That is the only moral of this entire story: law is the science-fiction of the present.

Notes

1. Boundas, '[Review of] Laurent de Sutter' and '[Review of] Alexandre Lefebvre'.
2. Mengue, *Deleuze et la question de la démocratie*.
3. See Patton, *Deleuzian Concepts*, 2–3. See also his 'Immanence, Transcendence, and the Creation of Rights'.
4. Chignola, 'Postfazione', and Amendola, 'Le fabbriche della triste legge'.
5. Lefebvre, *Image of Law*, xii.
6. See Žižek, *Organs without Bodies*, 189.
7. Moore, 'Book Review: *The Image of Law*'.

Bibliography

For a complete bibliography of Gilles Deleuze's writings, see Timothy S. Murphy, 'Bibliography of the Works of Gilles Deleuze', in Paul Patton, ed., *Deleuze: A Critical Reader*, 270–98 (Oxford: Blackwell, 1996), as well as David Lapoujade's 'Bibliographie générale des articles' in his editions of *L'île déserte* and *Deux régimes de fous* (Paris: Minuit, 2002 and 2003, respectively; the bibliography was not included in the English translations). A number of unpublished talks and lecture courses by Deleuze are available on *Web Deleuze*, edited by Richard Pinhas (<www.webdeleuze.com>). The entry on Deleuze in the *Stanford Encyclopedia of Philosophy* features a more comprehensive list of writings on Deleuze in English (<http://plato.stanford.edu/entries/deleuze/#Bib>).

Agamben, Giorgio, 'Absolute Immanence', in *Potentialities*, 220–39.

Agamben, Giorgio, 'Bartleby, or On Contingency', in *Potentialities*, 243–71.

Agamben, Giorgio, *Potentialities: Collected Essays in Philosophy*, ed. and trans. Daniel Heller-Roazen (Stanford: Stanford University Press, 2007).

Alliez, Éric, *Deleuze: Philosophie virtuelle* (Paris: Les Empêcheurs de penser en rond, 1996).

Alliez, Éric, *The Signature of the World, Or, What is Deleuze and Guattari's Philosophy?* trans. Eliot Ross Albert and Alberto Toscano (London: Continuum, 2004).

Alliez, Éric, ed., *Gilles Deleuze: Une vie philosophique* (Paris: Les Empêcheurs de penser en rond, 1998).

Alliez, Éric, et al., eds., *Gilles Deleuze: Immanence et vie* (Paris: PUF, 1998).

Amendola, Giso, 'Le fabbriche della triste legge', *Il Manifesto*, 10 December 2011.

Backès-Clément, Cathérine, 'Les Petites filles ou les aventures de la philosophie', in *Gilles Deleuze*, 17–21 (Paris: Inculte, 2005).

Badiou, Alain, *Deleuze: The Clamor of Being*, trans. Louise Burchill (Minneapolis: University of Minnesota Press, 2006).

Badiou, Alain, 'Deleuze's Vitalist Ontology', in *Briefings on Existence: A Short Treatise on Transitory Ontology*, ed. and trans. Norman Madarasz, 63–71 (Albany, NY: State University of New York Press, 2006).

Badiou, Alain, 'Gilles Deleuze: Sur *Le Pli: Leibniz et le baroque*', in Badiou, *L'aventure de la philosophie française depuis les années 1960*, 27–55 (Paris: La Fabrique, 2012).

Beaulieu, Alain, ed., *Gilles Deleuze: Héritage philosophique* (Paris: PUF, 2005).

Benveniste, Émile, '*Ius* and the Oath in Rome', bk. 5, ch. 3 of *Dictionary of Indo-European Concepts and Society*, trans. Elizabeth Palmer, 395–404 (Chicago: Hau, 2016).

Bergen, Véronique, 'A propos de la formule de Badiou, "Deleuze un platonicien involontaire"', in Stengers and Verstraeten, eds, *Gilles Deleuze*, 19–30.

Bergen, Véronique, *L'ontologie de Gilles Deleuze* (Paris: L'Harmattan, 2001).

Bouaniche, Arnaud, *Gilles Deleuze, une introduction*, rev. edn (Paris: Pocket, 2010).

Boundas, Constantin V., '[Review of] Alexandre Lefebvre, *The Image of Law: Deleuze, Bergson, Spinoza*', *Symposium: Canadian Journal of Continental Philosophy/Revue canadienne de philosophie continentale* 15, no. 2 (Summer 2011): 199–208.

Boundas, Constantin V., '[Review of] Laurent de Sutter, *Deleuze: La Pratique du Droit*', *Symposium: Canadian Journal of Continental Philosophy/Revue canadienne de philosophie continentale* 15, no. 1 (Spring 2011): 201–7.

Braidotti, Rosi, Claire Colebrook and Patrick Hanafin, eds., *Deleuze and Law: Forensic Futures* (Basingstoke: Palgrave Macmillan, 2009).

Bryant, Levi R., *Difference and Givenness: Deleuze's Transcendental Empiricism and the Ontology of Immanence* (Evanston, IL: Northwestern University Press, 2008).

Cacciari, Massimo, *Icone della legge*, 4th rev. edn (Milan: Adelphi, 2002).

Bibliography

Deleuze, Gilles, *Bergsonism*, trans. Hugh Tomlinson and Barbara Habberjam (New York: Zone Books, 1991).

Deleuze, Gilles, *Cinema 1: The Movement-Image*, trans. Hugh Tomlinson and Barbara Habberjam (Minneapolis: University of Minnesota Press, 2003).

Deleuze, Gilles, *Cinema 2: The Time-Image*, trans. Hugh Tomlinson and Robert Galeta (Minneapolis: University of Minnesota Press, 1989).

Deleuze, Gilles, *Da Cristo alla borghesia e altri scritti: saggi, recensioni, lezioni 1945–1957*, ed. Fabio Treppiedi and Giuseppe Bianco (Milano: Mimesis, 2010).

Deleuze, Gilles, 'Description of Woman: For a Philosophy of the Sexed Other', trans. Keith W. Faulkner, *Angelaki* 7, no. 3 (December 2002): 17–24.

Deleuze, Gilles, *Desert Islands and Other Texts, 1953–1974*, ed. David Lapoujade, trans. Michael Taormina (Los Angeles: Semiotext(e), 2004).

Deleuze, Gilles, *Difference and Repetition*, trans. Paul Patton (New York: Columbia University Press, 1994).

Deleuze, Gilles, *Empiricism and Subjectivity: An Essay on Hume's Theory of Human Nature*, trans. Constantin V. Boundas (New York: Columbia University Press, 1991).

Deleuze, Gilles, *Essays Critical and Clinical*, trans. Daniel W. Smith and Michael A. Greco (Minneapolis: University of Minnesota Press, 1997).

Deleuze, Gilles, *Expressionism in Philosophy: Spinoza*, trans. Martin Joughin (New York: Zone Books, 1990).

Deleuze, Gilles, *The Fold: Leibniz and the Baroque*, trans. Tom Conley (London: Continuum, 2006).

Deleuze, Gilles, *Foucault*, trans. and ed. Seán Hand (Minneapolis: University of Minnesota Press, 1988).

Deleuze, Gilles, *Kant's Critical Philosophy*, trans. Hugh Tomlinson and Barbara Habberjam (London: Athlone, 1984).

Deleuze, Gilles, *The Logic of Sense*, ed. Constantin V. Boundas, trans. Mark Lester with Charles Stivale (London: Athlone, 1990).

Deleuze, Gilles, *Masochism: Coldness and Cruelty* (New York: Zone Books, 2006).

Deleuze, Gilles, *Negotiations, 1972–1990*, trans. Martin Joughin (New York: Columbia University Press, 1995).

Deleuze, Gilles, 'Nietzsche', in *Pure Immanence*, trans. Anne Boyman, 53–102 (New York: Zone Books, 2001).

Deleuze, Gilles, *Nietzsche and Philosophy*, trans. Hugh Tomlinson (New York: Columbia University Press, 2006).

Deleuze, Gilles, *Proust and Signs: The Complete Text*, trans. Richard Howard (Minneapolis: University of Minnesota Press, 2000).

Deleuze, Gilles, *Sur Spinoza*, lecture course at Vincennes, lecture of 9 December 1980: 'La puissance, le droit naturel classique'. Available at: <https://www.webdeleuze.com/textes/9> (last accessed 6 May 2021).

Deleuze, Gilles, *Two Regimes of Madness: Texts and Interviews 1975–1995*, ed. David Lapoujade, trans. Ames Hodges and Michael Taormina (Los Angeles: Semiotext(e), 2006).

Deleuze, Gilles, and Félix Guattari, *Anti-Oedipus: Capitalism and Schizophrenia*, trans. Robert Hurley, Mark Seem, and Helen R. Lane (Minneapolis: University of Minnesota Press, 1983).

Deleuze, Gilles, and Félix Guattari, 'Balance-Sheet for "Desiring-Machines"', in Félix Guattari, *Chaosophy: Texts and Interviews 1972–1977*, ed. Sylvere Lotringer, trans. David L. Sweet, Jarred Becker and Taylor Adkins, 90–115 (Los Angeles: Semiotext(e), 2009).

Deleuze, Gilles, and Félix Guattari, *Kafka: Toward a Minor Literature*, trans. Dana Polan (Minneapolis: University of Minnesota Press, 1986).

Deleuze, Gilles, and Félix Guattari, *A Thousand Plateaus: Capitalism and Schizophrenia 2*, trans. Brian Massumi (Minneapolis: University of Minnesota Press, 1987).

Deleuze, Gilles, and Félix Guattari, *What is Philosophy?* trans. Hugh Tomlinson and Graham Burchell (New York: Columbia University Press, 1994).

Deleuze, Gilles, and Claire Parnet, *L'abécédaire de Gilles Deleuze*, 3 DVDs (Paris: Montparnasse, 2004).

Deleuze, Gilles, and Claire Parnet, *Dialogues II*, trans. Hugh Tomlinson and Barbara Habberjam, rev. edn (New York: Columbia University Press, 2007).

Derrida, Jacques, *Before the Law: The Complete Text of* Préjugés, trans. Sandra Van Reenen and Jacques De Ville (Minneapolis: University of Minnesota Press, 2018).

Derrida, Jacques, 'Force of Law: The "Mystical Foundation of

Authority"', trans. Mary Quaintance, in *Deconstruction and the Possibility of Justice*, ed. Drucilla Cornell, Michel Rosenfeld, and David Carlson, 3–67 (London: Routledge, 1992).

de Sutter, Laurent, 'Une pratique comique du droit est-elle possible?' *Revue interdisciplinaire d'études juridiques* 60, no. 1 (2008): 157–71.

de Sutter, Laurent, and Serge Gutwirth, 'Droit et cosmopolitique: Notes sur la contribution de Bruno Latour à la pensée du droit', *Droit & Société* 56–57, no. 1 (2004): 259–86.

de Sutter, Laurent, and Kyle McGee, 'Postscript: A Brief Reflection on the Universality of Jurisprudence', in de Sutter and McGee, eds, *Deleuze and Law*, 204–12.

de Sutter, Laurent, and Kyle McGee, eds, *Deleuze and Law* (Edinburgh: Edinburgh University Press, 2012).

Dosse, François, *Gilles Deleuze and Félix Guattari: Intersecting Lives*, trans. Deborah Glassman (New York: Columbia University Press, 2011).

Dworkin, Ronald, *Law's Empire* (Cambridge, MA: Belknap Press of Harvard University Press, 1986).

Foucault, Michel, *Discipline and Punish: The Birth of the Prison*, trans. Alan Sheridan, 2nd edn (New York: Vintage, 1995).

Foucault, Michel, 'Le grand enfermement', in *Dits et écrits*, ed. Daniel Defert and François Ewald, vol. 2, no. 105: 296–306 (Paris: Gallimard, 1994).

Foucault, Michel, 'Theatrum Philosophicum', trans. Donald F. Brouchard and Sherry Simon, in *Essential Works of Foucault, 1954–1984*, vol. 2: Aesthetics, Method, and Epistemology, ed. James D. Faubion, 343–68 (New York: New Press, 1997).

Gualandi, Alberto, *Deleuze* (Paris: Les Belles Lettres, 1998).

Hallward, Peter, *Out of This World: Deleuze and the Philosophy of Creation* (London: Verso, 2006).

Halsey, Mark, *Deleuze and Environmental Damage* (Abingdon: Routledge, 2017).

Hardt, Michael, *Gilles Deleuze: An Apprenticeship in Philosophy* (Minneapolis: University of Minnesota Press, 1993).

Jaeglé, Claude, *Portrait oratoire de Gilles Deleuze aux yeux jaunes* (Paris: PUF, 2005).

Jullien, François, *The Silent Transformations*, trans. Krzysztof Fijałkowski and Michael Richardson (London: Seagull, 2011).

Kant, Immanuel, *The Conflict of the Faculties*, trans. Mary J. Gregor and Robert Anchor, in *Religion and Rational Theology*, ed. Allen W. Wood and George Di Giovanni, 233–327 (Cambridge: Cambridge University Press, 1996).

Lacan, Jacques, 'Kant with Sade', in *Écrits: The First Complete Edition in English*, trans. Bruce Fink, Héloïse Fink and Russell Grigg, 645–68 (New York: Norton, 2005).

Landolfi, Claudia, *Deleuze e il moderno* (Rome: Aracne, 2012).

Lardreau, Guy, *L'exercice différé de la philosophie: A l'occasion de Deleuze* (Lagrasse: Verdier, 1999).

Latour, Bruno, *The Making of Law: An Ethnography of the Conseil d'Etat*, trans. Marina Brilman and Alain Pottage (Cambridge: Polity, 2010).

Latour, Bruno, 'Note brève sur l'écologie du droit saisie comme énonciation', *Cosmopolitiques*, no. 8: Pratiques cosmopolitiques du droit, ed. Frédéric Audren and Laurent de Sutter (December 2004): 34–40.

Lefebvre, Alexandre, 'Human Rights in Deleuze and Bergson's Later Philosophy', in de Sutter and McGee, eds, *Deleuze and Law*, 48–68.

Lefebvre, Alexandre, *The Image of Law: Deleuze, Bergson, Spinoza* (Stanford: Stanford University Press, 2008).

Martin, Jean-Clet, *Deleuze* (Paris: L'Eclat, 2012).

Martin, Jean-Clet, *Variations: The Philosophy of Gilles Deleuze*, trans. Constantin V. Boundas and Susan Dyrkton (Edinburgh: Edinburgh University Press, 2010).

Massumi, Brian, ed., *A Shock to Thought: Expression after Deleuze and Guattari* (London: Routledge, 2000).

Massumi, Brian, *A User's Guide to Capitalism and Schizophrenia: Deviations from Deleuze and Guattari* (Cambridge, MA: MIT Press, 1992).

McGee, Kyle, *Bruno Latour: The Normativity of Networks* (London: Routledge, 2014).

McGee, Kyle, ed., *Latour and the Passage of Law* (Edinburgh: Edinburgh University Press, 2016).

Mengue, Philippe, *Deleuze et la question de la démocratie* (Paris: L'Harmattan, 2003).

Mengue, Philippe, *Faire l'idiot: La politique de Deleuze* (Meaux: Germina, 2013).

Mengue, Philippe, *Gilles Deleuze ou le système du multiple* (Paris: Kimé, 1994).

Bibliography

Moore, Nathan, 'Book Review: *The Image of Law: Deleuze, Bergson, Spinoza*', *Law, Culture & the Humanities* 5, no. 3 (October 2009): 462–66.

Murray, Jamie, *Deleuze and Guattari: Emergent Law* (London: Routledge, 2012).

Mussawir, Edward, *Jurisdiction in Deleuze: The Expression and Representation of Law* (London: Routledge, 2011).

Nancy, Jean-Luc, 'Lapsus iudicii', in *A Finite Thinking*, trans. Simon Sparks, 152–71 (Stanford: Stanford University Press, 2003).

Ost, François, *Sade et la loi* (Paris: Odile Jacob, 2005).

Patton, Paul, 'Immanence, Transcendence, and the Creation of Rights', in de Sutter and McGee, eds, *Deleuze and Law*, 15–31.

Patton, Paul, *Deleuze and the Political* (London: Routledge, 2000).

Patton, Paul, *Deleuzian Concepts: Philosophy, Colonization, Politics* (Stanford: Stanford University Press, 2010).

Patton, Paul, ed., *Deleuze: A Critical Reader* (Oxford: Blackwell, 1996).

Rajchman, John, *The Deleuze Connections* (Cambridge, MA: MIT Press, 2000).

Rancière, Jacques, 'The Indecisive Affect', in *Dissenting Words: Interviews with Jacques Rancière*, ed. and trans. Emiliano Battista, 205–20 (London: Bloomsbury, 2017).

Riley, Patrick, *Leibniz' Universal Jurisprudence: Justice as the Charity of the Wise* (Cambridge, MA: Harvard University Press, 1996).

Rosset, Clément, 'Sécheresse de Deleuze [1972]', in *Faits divers*, 217–22 (Paris: PUF, 2013).

Saunders, David, 'Cases against Transcendence: Gilles Deleuze and Bruno Latour in Defence of Law', in de Sutter and McGee, eds, *Deleuze and Law*, 185–203.

Schérer, René, *Regards sur Deleuze* (Paris: Kimé, 1998).

Schiavone, Aldo, *The Invention of Law in the West*, trans. Jeremy Carden and Antony Shugaar (Cambridge, MA: Belknap Press of Harvard University Press, 2012).

Schmitt, Carl, *The Nomos of the Earth in the International Law of the Jus Publicum Europaeum*, trans. G. L. Ulment (New York: Telos Press Publishing, 2006).

Shaviro, Steven, *Without Criteria: Kant, Whitehead, Deleuze and Aesthetics* (Cambridge, MA: MIT Press, 2009).

Sibertin-Blanc, Guillaume, *Deleuze et l'Anti-Oedipe: La production du désir* (Paris: PUF, 2010).

Sibertin-Blanc, Guillaume, *Politique et État chez Deleuze et Guattari* (Paris: PUF, 2013).

Sloterdijk, Peter, *Critique of Cynical Reason*, trans. Michael Eldred (Minneapolis: University of Minnesota Press, 1987).

Stengers, Isabelle, 'Une pratique cosmopolitique du droit est-elle possible? Entretien avec Laurent de Sutter', in *Cosmopolitiques*, no. 8: Pratiques cosmopolitiques du droit, ed. Frédéric Audren and Laurent de Sutter (December 2004): 14–33.

Stengers, Isabelle, *La Vierge et le neutrino: Les scientifiques dans la tourmente* (Paris: Les Empêcheurs de penser en rond, 2006).

Stengers, Isabelle, et Pierre Verstraeten, eds, *Gilles Deleuze* (Paris: Vrin, 1998).

Tarde, Gabriel, *Les transformations du droit: Étude sociologique*, ed. Jean Milet (Paris: Berg International, 1994).

Tournier, Michel, *The Wind Spirit*, trans. Arthur Goldhammer (London: Methuen, 1991).

Villani, Arnaud, *La guêpe et l'orchidée: Essai sur Deleuze* (Paris: Belin, 2000).

Widder, Nathan, *Political Theory after Deleuze* (New York: Continuum, 2012).

Žižek, Slavoj, *Organs without Bodies: On Deleuze and Consequences*, 2nd edn (Abingdon: Routledge, 2012).

Žižek, Slavoj, *The Ticklish Subject: An Essay in Political Ontology* (London: Verso, 1999).

Zourabichvili, François, 'Deleuze et le possible', in Alliez, ed., *Gilles Deleuze*, 335–57.

Zourabichvili, François, *Deleuze, a Philosophy of the Event, together with The Vocabulary of Deleuze*, trans. Kieran Aarons, ed. Gregg Lambert and Daniel W. Smith (Edinburgh: Edinburgh University Press, 2012).

Printed and bound by CPI Group (UK) Ltd, Croydon, CR0 4YY

28/01/2025

01827105-0004